The GREATEST
in the WORLD

illustrated by
Graham Kennedy

Chris Jones & Brian Lee

The Greatest
DIY
Tips in the World

A 'The Greatest in the World' book

www.thegreatestintheworld.com

Illustrations:
Graham Kennedy

Typesetting:
BR Typesetting

Cover images:
© Chris Barrett; © Theresa Martinez; © Mats Tooming;
all courtesy of www.fotolia.com; © Clive Nichols

Copy editor:
Bronwyn Robertson
theartsva.com

Series creator/editor:
Steve Brookes

First published in 2005 by Public Eye Publications

This edition published in 2008 by
The Greatest in the World Ltd, PO Box 3182,
Stratford-upon-Avon, Warwickshire CV37 7XW

Text and Illustrations Copyright © 2008 – The Greatest in the World Ltd

A CIP catalogue record for this book is available from the British Library
ISBN 978-1-905151-62-2

Printed and bound in China by 1010 Printing International Ltd.

I would like to dedicate this book to my wonderful Mum and Dad, Thelma and Bill – they taught me well!

Also a special dedication to my ever-loving wife Cathy for years of encouragement and patience, and my two wonderful sons Peter & Mark.

Chris

With loving thanks to my daughter, Dawn, whose time and effort putting everything together on the PC neatly hid my lack of computer literacy!

A particular dedication, also, to my friend and work colleague Guy Burtenshaw without whose encouragement to join him and the team at shows around the UK my part in this book would never had happened.

Brian

Contents

Foreword by Steve Brookes ...

Many of us like to dabble at DIY from time to time and, if we are honest, with varying degrees of success. When I decided to add a DIY tips book to our expanding library of publications, I had no doubt in my mind who should write it!

It was during the late 90s, that I first met Chris and Brian, when I was touring the UK, presenting gardening shows on stage for a major DIY and garden store. They were presenting DIY demonstrations to audiences who would sit totally engrossed, being informed and entertained as Chris and Brian imparted their years of knowledge and expertise with flair and humour. Within a half-hour show they would have dispensed numerous tips and ideas and audience members would linger to dig for a little more advice and engage in conversation with these two likeable chaps. No-one ever walked away without a smile on their face!

What you see with Chris and Brian is exactly what you get – two sincere, genial tradesmen who really know their stuff. Both have had a lifetime of experience in all areas of DIY with Chris specialising in plumbing and electrics whilst Brian was up to his neck in paint and wallpaper. Between them they have also covered carpentry and general building. When I asked them to collaborate on a DIY tips book they fell about laughing – then, thankfully, they agreed!

The result is what you have before you now – a great little DIY tips book! It may not contain an answer to every DIY question you have but I can guarantee that you will pick it up and refer to it again and again. Maybe you want to work out how many rolls of wallpaper you need for the spare bedroom; how to easily filter lumpy paint or how to unblock a sink. It's all here. Now you can begin to enjoy your DIY.

Good luck!

Steve Brookes
Editor

"Tell a man there are 300 billion stars in the universe and he'll believe you. Tell him a bench has wet paint on it and he'll have to touch it to be sure."

Painting & wallpapering

chapter 1
Painting

Quality counts

It is always worth buying the best paintbrushes that you can afford as, with a bit of care, they can be used many times without the annoyance of the bristles falling out mid stroke. If possible, choose paintbrushes that have bristles with split ends as this means a quality brush! To add a little interest to your brush choosing it is worth noting that the bristles on 'pure bristle' brushes are taken from wild pigs or boars residing in China and India. The Chinese bristles are invariably black, very strong and premium quality. Indian pig bristles, in contrast, vary in colour, are coarser, longer and not so strong. Cheaper brushes contain a mixture of pig bristle and horsehair.

Storing brushes and rollers

Once you have finished washing your paintbrushes, give them a final rinse in fabric conditioner to keep them really soft. As soon as your paint brushes are completely dry spend some time running an old comb through the bristles to smooth them out and remove any loose ones. Brushes are best stored hanging down but only if the bristles can be supported and not allowed to rest on a surface otherwise they become permanently bent and misshapen. If you cannot achieve this, then wrap the bristles in tissue paper and hold them together with an elastic band. Paint rollers should be allowed to dry naturally, removed from their housings and handles, and stored on end.

Window masking

If you use strips of masking tape to protect window glass when painting the frames then be sure to remove it from the glass as soon as possible. If you leave it until the paint has completely dried you risk the chance of pulling off some of the new paint which will have dried across the edge of the tape. You may also get an adhesive residue left on the glass if you leave the tape there for too long.

Long painting jobs

If you cannot finish your painting job in one day and intend to continue the next morning, or if you have to stop painting for a short while, then don't bother washing out your brushes or rollers. Instead simply wrap them tightly in plastic kitchen wrap (cling-film) or aluminium kitchen foil to keep the air from drying out the paint and store them in a cool place. The next morning they will be ready to use immediately.

Dust-free door painting

A sheet of newspaper or cardboard placed under a door will prevent dust being picked up by the brush when painting. The use of two wooden or plastic door wedges, one each side, will keep the door firmly in position so that both sides can be easily painted.

Damp brushes are best

It is always best to dampen a brush before use as this will give a more even application of the paint. When using latex paints the brushes should be dampened with water whereas, for oil-based paints you should use paint thinner. Always use paper towels to remove excess water or thinner before using the brush.

Quick tip

WARM PAINT
Paint will be easier to apply with better coverage if you stand the tin of paint in a bowl of warm water for half an hour before use. This is especially useful for enamel paints which can thicken considerably on a cold day.

Paint samples

Always buy a few sample pots of paint before choosing a colour. Paint each sample onto the two sides of a corner of the room to be painted. The way a colour looks will change due to the way the light reflects off the painted surface. Using samples in a corner like this will allow you to see these differences.

Paint variations

Even though tins of paint are labelled as being the same colour, different batches of paint may vary slightly. To avoid any noticeable differences always buy enough paint to complete the whole job in one go and from the same batch. This should be clearly marked on the tins.

Paintbrush support

Tying a piece of string across the open top of a tin of paint will provide support for the wet brush as well as being a useful means to wipe off excess paint from the brush.

Paraffin brush cleaner

After using oil-based paints, brushes can be cleaned effectively using paraffin. Place the brushes in a jar of paraffin overnight. The paint from the brushes will fall to the bottom of the jar and the clear paraffin above can be re-used. Finally wash the brushes in warm, soapy water and dry well before storing.

Quick tip

LUMP-FREE PAINT

If you are using a tin of paint that has been used before and stored, it may still have a few lumps in it after stirring well. Avoid even the smallest lumps ruining your painting by taking the trouble to strain the paint through a pair of tights or stockings before use.

Paint kettle

Professional decorators usually transfer paint from the shop-bought tin into a smaller and more portable container with a handle called a 'paint kettle'. You will probably find it useful to do the same. It is a good idea to line the paint kettle with aluminium foil as you can throw this away when you have finished. This means that previously used paint doesn't contaminate the newer paint when you come to use the paint kettle again.

Soften your paintbrushes

If you find that the bristles of many of your paintbrushes have become a bit hard they can easily be softened by soaking them in hot, freshly boiled vinegar. When they have been restored to soft, useable brushes again wash well in soapy water before use.

Rescuing a paintbrush

If a paintbrush becomes rock hard with old paint and all other efforts have failed, there is still a chance that you can rescue it. This is good news, particularly if the paintbrush is a high quality one. First suspend the hard paintbrush for a day with its bristles submerged in raw linseed oil. Then, wearing rubber gloves, rinse the bristles in warmed turpentine solution, working with your fingers to remove all the loosened deposits of old paint. Finally rinse the brush well in warm, soapy water.

Suspending paintbrushes

Whenever you need to soak a paintbrush by suspending the bristles in a jar then attach two clothes pegs to the brush handle. These will rest on the lip of the jar and prevent the bristles from coming into contact with the bottom of the jar and becoming bent.

Reusable brush cleaner

After you have used brush cleaning fluid or turpentine don't be too quick to throw the dirty liquid away. If you allow the sediment to settle to the bottom of the jar overnight and then decant the clear liquid above you can reuse it the next time you need to clean paintbrushes.

Tiny paint jobs

For coping with very small paint jobs such as touching up marks and scratches, make a suitable tiny paint applicator by bending a pipe cleaner into a triangle.

Homemade cutting in brush

To paint awkward corners of a window frame or edges of a wall or ceiling requires a small brush with tapering bristles. These are called 'cutting-in' brushes and are available from the DIY store — some with angled bristles. If you have not got one then you can make your own quick version by simply fixing an elastic band tightly around the top of the bristles of an ordinary paintbrush (the smallest you have). This will bind the bristles closely together and allow you to paint those difficult places.

PAINT TIN LIDS

When you have finished using a tin of paint, smear a little Vaseline (petroleum jelly) around the lip of the lid before replacing. This will make it much easier to remove the next time you come to use it.

Spraying parts of a bicycle

If you are painting something awkwardly shaped, like a bicycle, and you don't want to paint all of it, protect with cling-film the areas that you don't want to cover and use a paint sprayer – it's much quicker. Do this outside, on a still day, with protection for the surface you are working on and for your breathing.

White-only paintbrushes

No matter how much you clean a brush after using coloured paint, there will still be a residue of paint left which can slightly discolour white paint. It is always best to keep a couple of brushes of different sizes specifically for white paint only.

Change brushes often

If you have a long painting job to undertake make sure that you change your brush every couple of hours. Using the same brush all day will eventually cause it to harden due to collected paint deep in the bristles and cleaning it will become very difficult.

Painting guttering

Although manufacturers don't usually recommend painting plastic gutters and downpipes, if you want to match them with other colours of your exterior décor you can paint them with two coats of exterior gloss paint of the appropriate colour. The trick is to brush the coats of paint out further than you would if painting a door.

Ladder painting

When painting up a ladder put the paint tin into a larger container, your paintbrush can then be put into the space around the smaller tin, leaving your hands free.

Storing paint

When you have finished with a tin of paint and want to store the remainder make sure the lid is on tight and turn it upside down for a few seconds before turning it back upright; this will allow for an airtight seal to form around the lid so that when you reuse the tin there won't be a thick skin on top of the paint. If you are sure that the lid is on tight and there is little chance of the tin of paint being moved a lot during storage then you can actually keep the tin in its upside down position.

Make sure that you label any tins of leftover paint with a line on the outside of the tin which quickly shows you the level of the paint inside. If you find that you only have small amounts of paint left then these can still be very useful for touching up. However, even a little air in a tin will dry up these small amounts of paint, so transfer them instead into small, airtight containers and label with the colour and area of the house.

"There's nothing to match curling up with a good book when there's a repair job to be done around the house."

Masonry paint preparation

When painting the outside walls of a house using masonry paint, never prepare the walls using a wire brush to rub down as tiny bits of steel wire from the brush may become embedded in the wall. Most masonry paints are water based and of course water and steel will give you rust. This is the cause of the brown lines often seen on exterior paintwork, where the paint has caused rust on nails in the wall or on wire from a wire brush.

Paint filter

If you have a tin of paint that has acquired a few lumps but you do not want to go to the trouble of decanting the whole tin then there is a simpler option. Cut a piece of fine wire mesh into a circle so it just fits into the top of the paint tin. Let this circular sieve drop slowly through the paint to the bottom of the tin. As it drops through it will push any lumps to the bottom leaving only nice liquid paint above and ready to use.

Dripping paint tin

If you find that you are a messy painter and you always seem to get drips of paint down the side of the tin then reduce the risk of getting the paint getting onto any surface by standing the tin on a paper plate.

Bent bristles

If the bristles of your paintbrush are bent because they have been squashed in storage, simply hold them in the steam of a boiling kettle of water for a few minutes then pull them gently back into shape. Take care as the bristles may be hot!

Door tops

Whenever you paint a door or door frame remember to paint the top as well. Even though this area will never be seen it is where dust often accumulates. Removing the dust is much easier if the wood has been painted with gloss paint.

Paint smells

Some people are badly affected by paint odours. Leaving an onion cut in half in the room will remove a vast proportion of the odour or, alternatively, try adding vanilla extract to the paint at a ratio 2 teaspoons to 4 litres. This really works well and does not adversely affect the paint.

Quick tip

CLEAN TAPS
Before you start applying emulsion to the walls or ceiling in the bathroom wrap the taps, shower head etc. in cling-film to keep them safe from drips of paint and your inevitable messy hands.

Glass protection

To stop any stray paint sticking to the glass when painting window frames, apply a film of Vaseline (petroleum jelly) to the vulnerable edge of the glass. When the paint is dry it can easily be rubbed off the protected surface. Alternatively protect the glass from paint by laying strips of dampened newspaper along the edges. This is easily removed when the painting has been completed.

Blistering paint

A common problem when painting exterior woodwork is that the paint blisters as it dries. This is caused by moisture becoming trapped under the paint film. This causes the paint to expand as it dries and as it can't move sideways it moves away from the surface causing a blister. The cure is to simply wait until the paint has dried, rub down the blister, make sure the surface to be painted is perfectly dry and start again.

A good rule is not to do any painting outside after 3.30pm as the temperature starts to drop and damp in the air will settle on all surfaces.

Painting stairs

When painting wooden stair treads remember to paint them alternately. Only when the first set of treads is completely dry should you paint the others. This will ensure that you will still be able to use the stairs (albeit very carefully!) during the decorating period.

Stripping old paint?

A good rule of thumb is to strip paint only when it is blistered or cracked, otherwise you are making unnecessary work for yourself. If it isn't affected like this then it only needs rubbing down and re-painting.

Matching filler

If you have cracks to fill in a wall before painting, mix a little of the paint with the filler you intend to use on the walls. When the filler dries it will be the same colour as the walls will be and the repairs will be invisible after one coat of paint.

Quick tip

MINI PAINT APPLICATOR
A useful way of coping with those fiddly paint jobs is to recycle a used shoe polish container. Wash out the sponge and the container and fill with emulsion.

Painting lead

When painting lead first rub the metal with the cut face of half a raw potato. The paint will then stay on the lead even though the lead expands and contracts.

Mini-rollers

A variety of neat little paint rollers can be made for painting pipes and other fiddly jobs by using a selection of ladies' foam hair rollers. Ask permission first!

"The most important
work you and I
will ever do will be
within the walls of
our own homes.

Painting outside woodwork

Painting outside surfaces can seem like a daunting job but in reality it is not that bad. Here are some useful tips...

- Badly cracked, flaking, blistering paint must be stripped off. The easiest way is to use a hot air stripper and a stripping knife.

- For safety, drop the hot, stripped paint into a bucket of water.

- Never use a blow torch or hot air gun near windows, especially those with metal frames, as there is a risk of cracking the glass. Instead use a chemical paint stripper after carefully reading the instructions on the tin or bottle.

- Rebates around the windows can be stripped using paint stripper and a special shave-hook.

- Never paint over cracked or loose putty. If it is in poor condition then hack it out with an old table knife and renew.

- After stripping off the paint from outside woodwork, repair any cracks using fillers then rub down with fine glass paper. It is now ready to undercoat and gloss or stain.

Sponge paint effects

For sponge painting an internal wall you will need:

- A bucket of water
- Natural sea sponge (synthetic won't do)
- Coloured emulsion (the more varieties, the better effect)
- A paint tray
- Some old newspaper or old wallpaper turned pattern down
- A roll of masking tape
- A brush

1. Pour emulsion into the tray to a depth of only 5 or 6 mm.
3. Drop the sponge into the bucket of water, remove and squeeze out most of the water.
4. Holding the sponge dab it into the emulsion in the tray.
5. Dab the paper you have stuck down until you start to transfer the texture of the sponge onto the paper.
6. Now dab the wall with the sponge until you need to reload with paint. Repeat the process until you have gone over the area you want with that particular colour.
7. Now drop the sponge into the bucket of water, change the paint colour in the tray and start all over again. Six to eight different colours looks really nice.
8. For an even finish use the same side of the sponge from the beginning to the end of the job.
9. Never allow another person to take over halfway through as their technique will always differ from yours regardless of how much tuition you give them!

"Success is very
often failure with
a new coat of paint."

Painting pipes

If you have to paint pipes that are fixed to a wall, cut out a piece of cardboard, place this behind the pipes to be painted and then paint them in the usual way. This will prevent any paint getting onto the wall behind.

Painting railings

An easy and quick way to paint railings etc. is to use a cheap car cleaning mitten! Dip your 'mittened' hand into the paint, take off any surplus, then grip the railing with the mitten and run your hand up and down. This is much less tedious than using a brush.

Quick tip

THINNING GLOSS PAINT

When using gloss paint it starts to go thick after a while and becomes more difficult to paint with. If this happens all you need do is add a generous squirt of washing-up liquid to the paint and give it a good stir. It will then go further, spread better and will not leave brush marks.

Painting tool kit

- Stiff brush (not wire)
- Polyester and lambs wool paint rollers and tray
- 12.5 cm (5") emulsion brush
- 1.25 cm (½") paintbrush
- 2.5 cm (1") paintbrush
- 5 cm (2") paintbrush
- Plumb line
- Sponge
- Bucket
- Ladder
- Paint kettles
- Wall scrapers
- Putty knife
- Masking tape
- Small screwdriver
- Protective sheets
- Wood and wall filler
- Sealant and application gun
- Putty
- Various grades of sandpaper and emery cloth

chapter 2
Wallpapering

Choosing wallpaper

Remember the following tips when choosing rolls of wallpaper:

- Rolls of similar wallpaper will always carry a 'batch number'. To complete a whole room, always choose rolls with the same batch number. Similar looking rolls of paper but with different batch numbers could have a slightly different colouring which isn't noticeable in the shop but will stick out like a sore thumb on the wall!

- A large, bold wallpaper pattern will always make a small room look even smaller.

- Light patterns on a light background will give the impression of space in a room.

- A small random pattern will help to camouflage bumpy or uneven walls.

- A striped pattern only looks really good when the surface is perfectly even.

Mixing wallpaper paste

When mixing wallpaper paste always make a stiff mix. Add the paste powder to cold water rather than water to the powder and stir with a piece of wood. This will avoid getting a lumpy mix. Leave for five minutes and put the wooden stick back in the middle of the bucket. If the stick stands up, then the mix is the correct consistency and is ready to use.

Removing wallpaper

Old wallpaper can be difficult to remove. A solution of equal parts vinegar and warm water, applied to the paper and allowed to soak in will make removal a lot easier. For more stubborn areas try increasing the amount of vinegar in the solution. Before attempting to remove wallpaper borders try loosening the strong adhesive with a hairdryer before using the vinegar and water solution.

Quick tip

CURLING CORNERS

If you find that you suffer the occasional curling of the corners of wallpaper but don't want to mix up a load of paste for the small job of re-sticking them, there is a quick and easy solution. Simply paint the back of the offending corner with egg-white and leave until tacky before pressing down firmly.

Starting to wallpaper

Always read the back of the wallpaper sleeve and follow the instructions to the letter. Even if you have hung wallpaper before, the particular paper you are hanging may need slightly different treatment. Always start hanging the paper by working away from the light source. This way you stand less chance of seeing the seams of the paper when it has dried. Remember that wallpaper paste is a powder mixed with water, so, when wallpapering around electric switches and electric sockets always turn off the power at the mains fuse box.

Measuring wallpaper

Make life easier when measuring lengths of wallpaper by using Blu-Tak to hold the top of the paper to the wall. This leaves both hands free to mark the correct length at the bottom.

Sealing paper joints

After you have finished wallpapering bathrooms or kitchens use a thin line of clear varnish to seal the paper joints which can peel in these often steamy environments.

Patching wallpaper

If you need to apply a patch to wallpaper, you can make the repair less noticeable by tearing the edges rather than cutting them. The joins with the rest of the paper are much less obvious.

Efficient pasting

When pasting wallpaper always adopt the 'herringbone' effect and move your pasting brush up the centre of the paper then from the centre to sides working from one end of the length of paper to the other. This will ensure an even and more efficient covering of the paste.

"If at first you don't succeed, remove all evidence that you ever tried."

Pasting bucket

When wallpapering, use a plastic mop bucket as a paste container. The pasting brush can be rested in the mop wringing section and any paste drips will fall back into the bucket.

Leftover wallpaper

Use leftover pieces of wallpaper to decorate different sized cardboard boxes. These can be used as attractive storage containers on top of wardrobes.

Quick tip

PATIENCE WHEN PAPERING

When pasting wallpaper, be a bit patient and leave the pasted paper to expand and contract for a few minutes before hanging (it should tell you how long on the wallpaper sleeve). This will stop the wallpaper joints opening and/or riding up when the paper has been hung.

Smoothing wallpaper

When you are hanging non-embossed wallpaper, instead of using a brush to smooth the paper onto the wall, try using a clean, dry paint roller.

Bubbly wallpaper

Even the most experienced decorator can suffer the agony of air bubbles in newly hung wallpaper. Remove these easily by cutting into each bubble with a sharp blade and inserting some paste into the hole using a syringe, then flatten gently to the wall using a wallpapering brush.

CLEANING A PASTE BRUSH
Always rinse a wallpaper pasting brush in salted water before washing it properly. This will remove the paste more easily and will help to leave the brush soft and springy.

Wallpapering finishing touches

When you have finished hanging the wallpaper wipe over any paintwork and wallpaper seams with a damp sponge – rinsing the sponge often in warm water. Finally, with a permanent felt tip pen, write on the top of the door frame how many rolls of wallpaper you used in that room - it we help you to remember in years to come!

Wallpapering tool kit

- Pasting table
- Pasting brush
- Craft knife
- Seam roller
- Long-bladed scissors
- Paperhanging brush
- Sponge
- Plumb line
- Spirit level
- Ruler
- Pencil
- Bucket
- Small pair of steps
- Blu-Tak

"People who say it can't be done should not interrupt those who are doing it."

Plumbing & electrics

chapter 3

chapter 3
Plumbing

Stop-cock knowledge

Make sure that all members of your household know the exact positions of the water stop valves in your house and how to turn them off in an emergency. Remember to open and close the valves once a year to make sure that they are working properly, and lubricate the taps if necessary with a few drops of oil to ensure that everyone can close them easily when required.

Quick tip

BATHROOM REPAIRS
Make sure that you put the plug in the sink or bath if you are doing any work on the taps, shower or anything involving small parts. If you don't, there is a good chance that a small part will invariably be lost down the plug hole!

Spotting a leaking pipe

If you are not sure of the location of a small leak in a pipe then cover the suspected area with very soapy water. Bubbles will instantly appear over the hole. This tiny leak can then be temporarily repaired by rubbing the area with Vaseline (petroleum jelly) and either tying a cloth around this part of the pipe or wrapping with plumber's tape. Remember this is not a permanent solution!

Fishy smell

Never ignore a fishy smell in a room. If no one has recently been cooking seafood then it could indicate an electrical fault which has resulted in the overheating and burning of plastic. Check all electrical appliances that are switched on. If the cause is not obvious then you may want to call in an electrician.

Blocked sink or bath

A blocked sink or bath waste pipe can usually be cleared by probing with a flexible piece of plastic curtain wire. This should quickly loosen and shift the blockage which must then be flushed away using a kettle of boiling water. To ensure that sink and bath waste pipes remain clear, periodically tip down a handful of baking soda followed by a cup of vinegar. This mixture should be left for an hour and then flushed away with copious amounts of boiling water. If all your efforts to unblock the kitchen sink have failed, try crumbling three Alka-Seltzer indigestion tablets into the plug hole and then pouring down a cup of white vinegar. If you wait for a few minutes then follow up with hot water, the sink should be clear.

"Automatic simply means that you can't repair it yourself.

Emergency pipe repair

An emergency repair of a burst pipe can be made using a length of garden hose. Split the hose down its length and wrap it around the damaged pipe. Secure the hose in place with three or more jubilee clips then call a plumber!

Copper pipe repair

A split copper pipe can be temporarily repaired by placing a matchstick or other sliver of wood over the split, covering with melted candle wax and wrapping up with plumber's tape.

Dripping taps

If you have an irritating dripping tap, don't fancy tackling it yourself and can't get a plumber for a day or so, then tie a piece of string around the end of the tap and dangle this into the plug hole. The dripping water will then flow silently down the string and into the drain.

Easier washers

When fitting new tap washers and 'O' sealing rings, first apply petroleum jelly to the washer, such as Vaseline. This will make the fitting easier and performance of the tap a lot better. Don't use oil, however, as this will attack and deteriorate the rubber.

Bath sealant

Baths always move slightly when they are filled with water. With this fact in mind always fill a bath with water before sealing around the edge with silicone sealant. This prevents the bath breaking away from the sealant due to the weight of the water.

New pipes

When adding new pipes to a plumbing system lay horizontal pipes so that they fall away slightly from the main vent pipe, to ensure that any air bubbles can easily escape.

Bleeding radiators

When bleeding radiators use a cloth wrapped around the venting hole as you slowly turn the key to release the trapped air. This will avoid leaving a dirty water stain on the wall if the water suddenly reaches the hole and spurts out. Never remove the valve plug completely as there is little chance of you reinserting it before the water squirts out!

Leaking cistern

To check if a toilet cistern is leaking, add some food colouring to the water in the cistern. After 20 minutes check the toilet bowl. If there is colouring in the water then the cistern has a leak.

Leaky overflow

If you have a leaky cistern overflow and can't get it fixed immediately temporarily stop the leak by tying a wooden spoon to the ballcock arm and place it across the sides of your cistern.

Summer heating check

It may not be something that you would immediately think of but always run you central heating system at least once during the summer time, as this will help to keep the pump impeller free and avoid winter problems.

Dealing with a frozen pipe

In the winter months many people experience problems triggered by the cold weather. Knowing how to deal with a freeze before it bursts a pipe or fitting can save a lot of mess and upset. Of course, a lot of problems with cold weather can be eliminated by making sure all plumbing is suitably insulated.

This guide, however, should help you get out of difficulty should you be faced with a freeze...

- If a pipe freezes, turn off the mains water supply at the stop valve inside your home, if fitted — these are often sited under the kitchen sink. If there isn't an internal valve, turn off the water at the external valve, which may be under a cover in your garden or path.

- Identify the location of the freeze. By checking the flow of water from all appliances, it should be possible to narrow down the position of the freeze.

- If the frozen pipe runs from a storage cistern and is not controlled by a valve, check that it hasn't split. If it has, empty the cold-water storage cistern either by opening the cold water taps and flushing the toilet or by siphoning the water from the cistern with a garden hose, then call your plumber.

- If any part of the hot water system is frozen, there could be a risk of explosion if the boiler (or other heat source) is kept alight, so ensure it is turned off or, for solid fuel systems, extinguish the fire.

- Once the section of pipe has been identified, you may be able to narrow down the exact point further by looking for clues. Possible causes are draughts from air vents next to pipework, an unlagged section of pipe, or pipework next to a vent in the roofspace.

- Before attempting to thaw the blockage, inspect the pipe and any nearby fittings. It is possible that the pipe may have split, or the fittings may have been pushed apart by the expansion of the ice. In this case, melting the ice will result in a leaking joint. If you find such damage, the water supply to this section should be turned off first, and preparation made to contain the leaking water.

- Open the tap on the affected pipe to allow water to flow as soon as the ice begins to thaw.

- If you are unsure as to the location of the ice blockage on the length of pipe, always start nearest to the tap and gradually work away from it.

- Apply heat gently to the affected area using a hairdryer or hot water bottle. A hair dryer, however, should only be used if you are certain that the pipe/joints are not damaged or split. Never use an electrical appliance in the vicinity of water. If you use a blowtorch, guard against fire and apply only very gentle heat. Excessive heating will cause soldered joints to melt and fail.

If you suspect that there might be a split in the pipe or joint then take precautions for water leakage in case the frozen area thaws out, and seek assistance from a plumber. As with all DIY, give safety top priority – if in doubt, get professional help.

"If at first you don't succeed, remove all evidence that you ever tried.

Plumbing tool kit

- Adjustable spanner
- Pipe wrench
- Water pump (slip-joint) pliers
- Plunger
- Hacksaw
- Blowtorch
- Soldering iron, solder and flux
- Pipe cutter
- Knife
- Emery cloth
- Plumbers tape (PTFE or Teflon tape)
- Radiator key
- Assortment of tap washers
- Pipe jointing compound

chapter 4
Electrics

NEW RULES FOR ELECTRICAL SAFETY

When? Since 1st January 2005 people carrying out electrical work in homes and gardens in England and Wales will have to follow new rules in the Building Regulations.

Where? The new rules apply to dwelling houses and flats including gardens and outbuildings such as sheds, detached garages, and greenhouses.

Why? These rules have been introduced to reduce the number of deaths, injuries, and fires caused by faulty electrical work and to make it harder for 'cowboy builders' to leave electrical installations in an unsafe condition.

What? Small jobs such as the provision of a socket-outlet or a light switch on an existing circuit do not need to be notified to the Building Control department of your local council. There are, however, exceptions for high risk areas such as kitchens and bathrooms.

All work that involves adding a new circuit to a dwelling, or electrical work in kitchens and bathrooms will need to be either notified to Building Control with a building regulation application, or carried out by a competent electrician who is registered with a Part P Self-Certification Scheme.

Information about new rules

The Building Control Department of your local district council can provide you with a full explanation of exactly which DIY electrical work is covered by the new rules, often in the form of a chart depicting the different examples of work in table format. Alternatively a free 'Explanatory Booklet on the Building Regulations' is published by the Government and is available by telephoning 0870 1226 236 or visiting **www.odpm.gov. uk/explanatory-booklet**.

Locating cables

When running an electrical cable under floorboards try using a mirror and torch to locate the cable under the floor. Before you start feeding cables through walls and under floors make a small hook from a piece of a wire coat hanger and push this into the end of the cable. When you can see the cable but cannot quite reach it, there is a chance that you can locate the hook on the end of the cable using another wire coat hanger and pull the cable through.

Wiring a plug

When you look at the inside of a UK plug the contact at the top is always used for the earth wire, if required. But what about the other two connections? Which is for live and which is for neutral? Well, a good way of remembering is that the neutral or bLue wire goes to the left connection (L for left) whilst the live or bRown wire goes to the right connection (R for right).

FUSE TESTING

To test a fuse use a torch with the battery cover end removed. Hold the fuse with one end touching the battery and the other touching the torch casing. If the bulb lights when you switch on the torch, then the fuse is OK.

Fuse replacement

If a fuse blows ALWAYS replace it with one of the same rating. Don't be tempted to use a 13amp fuse to replace a lower rated fuse, even as a temporary measure, because you will probably forget to change it and the appliance will be unsafe. It is also very important to try to find out why the fuse blew in the first place.

● For appliances up to 700w the fuse should be 3amp.

● For appliances between 700w and 1200w the fuse should be 5amp.

● For appliances over 1200w the fuse should be 13amp.

Light fittings

Due to the heat from an electric light bulb, over a period of time it can become extremely difficult to unscrew the plastic components on light fittings when it becomes necessary to change the shade etc. Running an ordinary pencil point over the threads before initial assembly will make future dismantling effortless. The graphite from the pencil point is a good heat resisting lubricator.

Top electrical safety tips

The Electrical Safety Council is keen to give you advice on taking sensible precautions to avoid the thousands of electrical fires and accidents that occur each year so that you and your family will be safe around the house and garden. Please heed the following tips:

- Get into the habit of turning off electric games and appliances when they're not in use and when you go to bed. It is not only safer, but will save you money and is kinder to the environment.

- Electrical items that are not in regular use should be switched off at the plug when you are away from the house for any length of time.

- Ensure any electrical items are approved standard when purchasing and keep them correctly maintained where necessary. Look for the BEAB seal of approval.

- Don't overload sockets – always try to use one plug to each socket and if you do have to use an adaptor, use a 'bar type' one with a fuse. Keep the total output of all plugs in the adaptor to no more than its rating (normally 13 amps). Remember, a kettle alone uses 13 amps!

- Never plug adaptors into adaptors and avoid using adaptors filled with plugs where possible.

- Get yourself an RCD (residual current device) – a simple piece of equipment that will cut off power and prevent you getting an electric shock. You can get one fitted to your fuse box, or buy a portable one and remember to use it – especially for outdoor jobs such as mowing the lawn.

- Regularly check the state of plugs, sockets, and flexes for signs of scorching or fraying. If you find a problem get the item repaired by a registered electrician.

- Don't put leads and cables under carpets or mats. It's not only a trip hazard, but could cause damage to the wiring.

- Don't remove a plug from a power point by pulling on the cord; pull the plug instead.

- Use covers on sockets accessible to young children.

- Use the correct wattage light bulb for all light fittings.

- Don't let leads from appliances or toasters trail across your cooker tops. This is a potential fire hazard. Also don't retrieve toast stuck in a toaster whilst it is plugged in, and especially not with a metal knife.

- Don't hammer in nails or drill holes in your walls unless you know what is behind the plaster – a nail through a live wire is potentially fatal.

- Liquids and electricity don't mix. Make sure your hands are dry before you use any electrical equipment and never keep water, drinks, or other liquids on or near electrical equipment. For example, don't put your cup of coffee on the microwave or a vase of flowers on the TV. And don't fill up the steam iron or the kettle while it's still plugged in.

- Never take mains powered electrical appliances into the bathroom, such as hair dryers, hair straighteners or radios.

Don't let the kids go straight from the paddling pool into the house (where there are electrical sources) without getting them dried first.

Extending cables

If you accidentally cut cables short when fixing a socket or switch and they won't reach the terminals don't panic. Use a strip of plastic block connectors and extend with lengths of the correct size cables, making sure there is enough room for the connectors.

Broken bulb

Sometimes, when you come to remove a light bulb that has blown, the bottom of the bulb becomes broken and is left stuck in the base of the lamp holder. First turn off the power and then carefully push a carrot into the remainder of the broken bulb. Use this as a handle to twist out the broken bulb base, and then discard it safely.

Cable hole

If you have to drill a hole in wood to pass through an electrical cable always ensure that you drill in the direction the cable is going to run. The cable will then run smoothly through the hole without getting snagged. If you need to pass a cable through a tight space then rub the length with car wax first and it should slip through easily.

Difficult plug

If an electric plug becomes difficult to insert or remove from the socket then try rubbing the metal contacts of the plug with a soft, graphite pencil. Graphite is a natural lubricant and you should find that the plug will slide effortlessly in and out of the socket!

Electrical tool kit

- Torch
- Pliers
- Sharp knife
- Wire cutters / stripper
- Insulated terminal screwdriver
- Neon test screwdriver
- Electrical insulation tape
- Assorted plastic connector blocks
- Assorted fuses
- Assorted cable ties
- Fuse wire
- Spare 3 pin plugs
- Spare cable:

    1.0mm for lighting circuits

    2.5mm for power circuits and immersion heater

    6.0mm for cooker circuits and showers up to 8.5kw

    10.0mm for cooker circuits and showers over 8.5kw

> Every DIY job is
> a self-portrait of the
> person who did it.

General décor
& DIY

chapter 5
General décor & DIY

Essential tool kit

The basic, essential tool kit for every house should include:

- Screwdrivers – both cross-head and flat blade, or an electric screwdriver with a variety of heads
- Allen keys
- Claw hammer
- Wooden mallet
- Tape measure
- Small adjustable spanner
- Plumber's wrench or large adjustable spanner
- Pliers (with built-in wire cutter / stripper)
- Wood chisel
- Torch (with batteries that work – check regularly!)
- Protective goggles
- Electrical tape
- Plumber's tape
- Small hacksaw
- Selection of nails, screws and plastic fixing plugs
- Selection of different glues – epoxy, wood and PVA
- Spare light bulbs, candles and matches

Child safety

Keep all DIY tools out of the reach of children. The kids may have watched you doing DIY and decide to have a go themselves. The results could be disastrous – for the kids and your house!

Decorating conditions

Natural daylight and good ventilation are the ideal conditions for decorating. If you have central heating then turn it off as the heat from radiators can cause uneven drying of paint and wallpaper paste. Circulating air through a room is the best for drying any decorated surface.

Non slip drilling

When drilling into potentially slippery surfaces such as metal or ceramic tiles, first stick a piece of masking tape onto the surface over the spot where you want to drill. This should prevent the drill bit from slipping. For tiles use a glass drill bit instead of a masonry bit. If the hole you need to drill is over 6mm in diameter then drill a pilot hole with a smaller drill bit. Never use the hammer action on a drill, you may crack the tile.

Quick tip

FILL IN STAGES

If you have large, deep holes or cracks to fill in plaster then be patient and do the job in two stages. Half fill first and leave to dry before completing the job. This way you will ensure even drying of the filler and avoid surface cracking later on.

Faster filing

A file is one of those tools which, if it's not cared for and stored correctly can become pretty useless. Here are a few tips for keeping your files up to scratch:

- Always protect your files from contamination by water or grease which can make them less effective and from getting knocked and chipped. For these reasons it is a good idea to keep your files in your toolbox wrapped in a cloth.

- Regularly use a wire brush to keep the grooves of your files clean and work along the grain of the file rather than against it.

- Filing aluminium can be tricky as the metal filings soon get stuck in the teeth of the file. To avoid this happening, coat the file in paraffin or rub some blackboard chalk over the teeth of the file before filing.

- If your file's teeth do become clogged then either roll a small ball of putty or Blu-Tak over the grooves to remove any small particles, or stick a piece of masking tape firmly over the file and rub it down into the grooves. When you peel the tape off any particles that were stuck in the grooves of the file will then be stuck to the tape!

Lining paper

Using lining paper is a great way of hiding any small blemishes, particularly on walls that have seen lots of filling work and other repairs. The paper can then be painted or used as a base for wallpapering. If the surface is to be wallpapered then the lining paper should always be hung horizontally to avoid the coinciding of paper joints and to give the best possible bonding strength.

Quick tip

CLEANING SHOWER HEADS

Mineral deposits from the water can eventually collect inside a shower head rose and block the outlet holes. To clean the rose, remove it and soak overnight in a bowl of vinegar. A needle or piece of fine wire can be used to clear the more stubborn deposits from holes. Before reassembling, rinse the rose well in cold water. Run the shower for a while before use.

Safe saw

When you buy a wood saw, many will not come with any protection for the teeth of the saw other than the cardboard wrapper. Storing a saw without the teeth covered is bad for the saw and dangerous for you! You can make a protective sleeve by splitting a length of rubber garden hose and putting this over the teeth or cutting a 2.5 cm (1") wide strip of tongue and groove flooring, placing the saw's edge in the groove and securing to the saw blade with rubber bands.

Blu-Tak on wallpaper

If the kids have put up posters in their bedrooms using Blu-Tak, removing it can be a problem and may tear the wallpaper. It will, however, come off the paper really easily if you first warm it for a few seconds with a hairdryer.

Battery care

Batteries kept in a warm environment will quickly lose their charge so ensure that they are kept in a cool place. Rechargeable batteries should always be recharged immediately after use and should never be stored in a 'flat' state. Even fully charged batteries should be recharged every two months if they are not being used.

Beware cheap tools

This may sound patently obvious but it is worth saying. When it comes to buying tools you really do get what you pay for. Cheap tools may seem like a good bargain but ultimately they will either let you down or give you below par performance. Buy the very best you can, even if you have to wait a while. You will then have tools that you will be more inclined to look after and hence they will last much longer.

Rust-free tools

Tool boxes stored in garages and sheds may get damp inside which could lead to rusting of tools. A few small packets of silica gel (such as those often found in the packaging of electrical goods) or mothballs placed in the tool box will absorb any moisture in the air and prevent rust formation.

Fitting positions

When decorating it is useful to remember the positions of wall fittings so that you can easily find the plugged holes to refit them after the job is finished, instead of poking around with a small screwdriver. This can be easily done by pushing matchsticks into the holes as soon as you remove the fittings. Then you simply push the matchsticks back through newly hung wallpaper as the holes they make will be hidden by the replaced fitting.

Cleaning paintwork

To clean paintwork you often need something that will do the job without scratching the paint surface. An old bath loofah, cut into pieces and used with detergent, is ideal for the job. The best liquid to use for cleaning white paint is easily made by boiling a few onions in three pints of water until soft. Drain off the water and use it with soap to clean the paintwork.

Repairing holes in vinyl

Small holes in a vinyl or linoleum floor can be repaired by using a wax crayon. Find a crayon of a similar colour to the floor and melt it carefully over the hole using a lighter, match or blowtorch, taking care not to blacken the wax by getting the flame too close. Allow the melted wax to drip into the hole and, when hardened, use a sharp blade to scrape off any that is proud of the floor.

Removing adhesive hooks

Sometimes when you try to remove a self-adhesive hook from a door it will take paint and maybe the surface of the wood with it! This can be avoided by first warming the hook with a hairdryer, which will loosen the glue and enable the hook to be prised off with a blunt knife. Any glue that remains on the door can be removed using white spirit.

GROUTING TILES

When applying grout between tiles, cotton wool buds are very useful. Excess cement is gathered up by the soft heads and they leave smooth lines. They will also reach into those awkward corners where your fingers or other grouting tools may fail.

Bent drill bit

A small drill bit that has become bent can be straightened by the following method. Sandwich the bit between two pieces of smooth hardwood, with the bottom piece securely clamped in a vice or work bench. Now repeatedly roll the top piece of wood backwards and forwards over the bit with strong pressure.

One only needs two tools in life: WD-40 to make things go, and duct tape to make them stop.

Overhead power

If you are rearranging a workshop or garage and thinking about installing more power sockets, then consider putting some in the ceiling positioned over the area where you will be using power tools. These sockets can be more accessible than wall mounted ones and will eliminate tripping over trailing cables.

Sticking shuttering

If you are laying areas of concrete you may need to make a retaining edge to the areas from pieces of wooden board called shuttering. When the concrete has set the boards are removed and the result is a nice flat edge to the concrete. Sometimes, however, the concrete will stick to the boards making them almost impossible to remove. To avoid this happening, coat the side of the board that will be in contact with the concrete with engine oil before use.

Quick tip

FREE RUNNING TAPE

A steel measuring tape will last much longer if it is always retracting smoothly without rubbing. To keep it in this good condition, apply a small spot of car wax onto the tape and wipe it along the length of the tape with a clean cloth. This will protect the tape surface and keep it running smoothly. Remember to repeat this tip after prolonged use of the tape especially if it is being used in a dusty environment.

Drill depth

Judging just how deep to drill can be difficult once you start drilling. Gauge the depth easily by marking the drill bit at the correct place with a coloured crayon, rubber band or masking tape. When your marker reaches the surface of the wood or masonry you know that the hole is the correct depth.

Concrete paths

If you lay a concrete path or patio, do not leave the surface smooth as it could become slippery and dangerous when wet. Before the concrete has set completely, pat gently across the whole surface with the thin edge of a piece of timber. This will create grooves in the surface of the concrete and the resulting set surface will be a lot safer.

Cooler drilling

When drilling into masonry a drill bit can get overheated and cause damage to the bit or the drill itself. Avoid this problem by withdrawing the tip every few seconds and allowing it to cool slightly before continuing. Alternatively, with a small spray bottle, squirt water into the hole periodically during drilling.

Quick tip

SHARPER SEWING NEEDLES
If you find that your sewing machine needles are becoming blunt, they can be easily sharpened by making a few stitches through a piece of emery cloth!

Rusted screws

Rusted-in screws, such as those in door hinges, can be loosened by first scraping paint and rust from around them and across the slots and then applying a little release oil. After leaving for half an hour touch the top of each rusted screw with the tip of a hot soldering iron. The heat from the soldering iron should expand the screw and break the rust's hold. The previously applied oil will ensure that the screw should now be easy to remove using a tight-fitting screwdriver.

Quick tip

REMOVING CEILING PAPER
When taking paper off a ceiling, first put a bin liner over the back of the step ladder into which the bits of paper can be placed as soon as they are removed. This saves a lot of cleaning up at the end of the day and bits of paper being trodden all over the house!

Firmer screws

If screws seem to be always working loose then you can ensure a firmer fix by removing the screws and dipping the threaded tips in either PVA glue, nail varnish or oil based paint. This is a particularly good tip to use when putting together flat-packed furniture, where many of the screw holes are pre-drilled.
The screws can often work loose, especially if the furniture is moved around.

Shabby sash cords

When you are renovating or just painting a genuine sash window the white cord can often spoil the final look of the job by appearing shabby and off colour. To avoid having to go to the trouble of replacing the sash cord simply coat it with white canvas shoe dye. This is obtainable with a sponge applicator making it easy to apply to the cord.

Dusty drilling

When drilling into a wall you will inevitably get brick dust falling everywhere and it is not always possible to protect every surface from getting covered, especially in awkward places. There are a few ways to solve the problem. Get an assistant to hold a vacuum cleaner nozzle close to the end of the drill bit as you are drilling. Alternatively tape an open envelope or even a dustpan to the wall just below your drill position to catch the brick dust.

Quick tip

MAGNETIC STORAGE
Every tool box eventually ends up with small screws and nails rattling around. Keep these tidy by sticking them to a small magnet as a temporary measure. When you get around to tidying up your tool box, all these oddments will be together ready for sorting and filing away in the correct places.

Easier hand cleaning

Before beginning painting or any other potentially messy DIY job, rub hair conditioner or Vaseline (petroleum jelly) over your hands. Dirt and grime are less likely to stick to your skin. After you have finished your task you should find it is much easier to wash everything off your hands with just soap and warm water.

This is particularly useful as some of the commercially available products for removing paint from skin can cause irritation. Cooking oil, however, will remove most paint from skin without any adverse effects and even window cleaning liquid is also pretty good at removing paint from your hands. After washing everything away, a good skin moisturiser is all that is required to prevent chapping and to keep your hands in good condition.

Homemade level

If you are putting up a shelf and you don't have a spirit level then it is easy to make your own temporary one. Fill a glass two-thirds full with water and stand it on a surface that you know is perfectly level (a kitchen worktop will usually suffice). When the water is dead still in the glass, mark the position of its surface on the glass with a marker pen. Now when you come to put up your shelf you can use the glass of water to ensure it is perfectly level.

Spanners

Always use the correct size spanner when undoing nuts. Using an ill-fitting or adjustable spanner can round off the nut making it difficult to use next time. If you don't have the correct size spanner then use one slightly larger and introduce a 'shim' such as a 1p or a 5p piece, between the spanner head and the nut. The shim may need to be tapped into place with a hammer for a really good tight fit.

Interior damp

One chore which should never be put off until another day is treating interior damp. If left it can become a serious hazard and more costly to correct. Here are some exterior causes of interior dampness and simple remedies:

- Sagging / broken gutter – replace
- Blocked downpipe hopper – clean out regularly
- Cracked downpipe – replace
- Cracked rendering – renew rendering
- Faulty pointing – cleanout and re-point
- Porous bricks – give two coats of water repellent brick sealant

Clean drill holes

If you try to insert a Rawlplug into a freshly drilled hole in masonry, often it will not penetrate far enough due to a blockage of drill dust from the brickwork. Get into the habit of cleaning the dust from the hole first by blowing into it using a bendy type of drinking straw.

DRILL BIT STORAGE

To avoid any loose drill bits becoming lost or damaged, keep them in an old hard spectacle case to protect them. This also serves as a handy way of carrying the drill bits in your pocket without making holes.

Pre-winter tasks

Remember the following and make the winter more manageable:

- Stock up on salt or grit to cope with icy paths and drives.

- Invest in a snow shovel – just in case!

- Make sure that doors and windows are well-fitting and sealed to minimise drafts. Consider hanging longer or thicker curtains to improve insulation.

- Check that all pipes are sufficiently lagged to minimise the risk of freezing.

- Check on loft insulation to see that it is all in place and sufficiently thick to do a good job.

- If you have an open fire then get the chimney swept well in advance of the constant use that it will get over the cold period.

- Have the central heating boiler serviced before it decides to break down just as the big freeze hits town!

Soldering tips

- To keep the tip of your soldering iron clean during use, regularly rub it over a piece of steel wool stapled to your workbench.

- So that you always have a piece of solder wire handy when you need it, wrap a length around the electrical cable of the soldering iron or clip a piece to the iron with a large bulldog clip.

- When soldering small parts together try using magnets, plasticine or Blu-Tak to hold them in place.

- So that you can see every tiny hole in a metal bucket that needs soldering, shine a light under the container and the places where solder is required will be clearly visible.

Tool belt

When working on a DIY task that requires a number of different tools then use a tool belt to carry them - either strapped to your waist or, if you are working off the ground, tied around the upper part of the ladder. Tools placed on the top of a stepladder are often out of view and therefore dangerous.

Quick tip

STORING MANUALS

Instruction manuals for DIY tools and other appliances around the home should always be kept together for easy reference. A small, old suitcase, that can be kept easily accessible, serves as a useful storage place.

Plasterboard

When cutting plasterboard there is no need to blunt your good saw or use a power tool. Simply score one side with a trimming knife, snap along the scored line then carefully turn the sheet over and score and snap along the other side. The result is just like a perfect cut!

When fixing plasterboard to a ceiling and you have no available help, then make up two T-shaped props so they fit just under the plasterboard surface when it is in position. These will be invaluable in keeping the board in place while you fix the screws or nails.

Ladder angle

A ladder should always be leaned against a wall or other surface so that the foot of the ladder is one measure out for every four measures in height. So for a 3.5 m (12') ladder its base should be 90 cm (3') out from the wall. If you are ever uncertain about whether your ladder is positioned correctly always get the help of someone else who can stand at the bottom and hold or 'foot' the ladder for you.

String dispenser

If you can never find the ball of string when you need it, or when you do it is always knotted up then try this. Get a small plastic funnel and fix it to the wall of the shed or garage so that it stays in an upright position. Place the ball of string in the top of the funnel threading the loose end through the narrow bottom. Your string it is always to hand and knot free.

Woodworm treatment

If you discover that you have woodworm in floors then these should be treated both on top and underneath the floorboards for effective control. Remove a few boards and, wearing a protective face mask and goggles, use a garden type pump-up sprayer with a curved lance to spray the affected timber.

Quick tip

HOMEMADE TILE GLUE

This may seem like an odd tip but it really works! If a wall tile falls off and you have no tile glue in the house, you can make your own using some jam. Heat the preserve to boiling point and apply to the back of the fallen tile using a paintbrush. Push the tile into place and hold it for a few minutes and you will find it will stick fast. Grout as normal and no-one will ever know!

Sinking ladder

When using a ladder on soil outside, there is always a chance that it could slip or sink into the ground. Standing the ladder on a board will help to avoid this happening. To be really sure of no slipping, nail a piece of wood across the board and place the ladder on the board so that the piece of wood wedges against it and stops the ladder from slipping backwards away from the wall.

Perfect right angle

To get an exact 90° angle, take three lengths of straight timber – 914 mm (3 ft), 1219 mm (4 ft) and 1524 mm (5ft). Nail or screw these together to make a triangle ensuring that the finished side lengths are as stated above. As long as your measuring is accurate, this will result in a true 90° corner. The other two angles will be 30° and 60°. You will then have a useful and decent sized right angle for many uses around the house and garden.

Wood drilling

- Always use a proper wood drill bit for drilling into timber. Masonry or metal drilling bits will often heat up and scorch the wood. The smell might be pleasant but the look of the wood surface may be marred.

- If using a large wood drill bit to drill a deep hole into timber then withdraw it occasionally to keep the hole free and prevent the bit getting jammed with wood dust.

- Always drill pilot holes in wood before trying to fix screws in order to stop the wood from splitting.

Loose leg

A loose wooden chair leg can be secured by removing it from the base of the chair and wrapping the loose end with a small strip of nylon, elasticated stocking. Then apply strong epoxy wood glue to both the stockinged end and the hole in the base of the chair before re-inserting.

Power tool protection

When using power tools inside or outside, always use a plug-in Residual Current Device (RCD). This will protect you from electrocution should you damage the cable on the power tool or should any fault occur during use.

Quick tip

SQUEAKY HINGES

If you have a squeaking door then try using Vaseline (petroleum jelly) to lubricate the hinges. This will work just as well as oil and won't run down the paintwork or drip onto the carpet.

Creaking stairs

The irritating noise of creaking stairs can be silenced by using PVA glue. First, with a chisel, prise a small gap between the creaking stair board and the riser. Then, using a piece of cardboard as a spreader, fill the gap with PVA glue.

Splitting wood

To prevent wood splitting when hammering in a nail use a very small drill to make a guide hole in the wood. This need only be a very tiny hole to do the trick. If the hole is too large then the nail will not provide the required firm fixing. Alternatively, if you haven't got a small drill then simply blunt the sharp end of the nail first and this will help to prevent splitting.

Loose fixing plug

If the hole that you have drilled for a plastic fixing plug is slightly too wide then don't risk the fixing not being completely secure because of the loose plug. Put some filler in the hole first and push the Rawlplug into this so it is flush with the surface, removing any excess filler that oozes out. Let it set before driving home the screw.

Hard putty

If stored putty has hardened, soften it by putting it into a plastic bag and placing it into a bowl of hot water for a time. An occasional squeeze will tell you when it is usable. To avoid this happening always store unused putty by wrapping it completely in aluminium kitchen foil.

Dust catcher

When drilling overhead you will no doubt get bits of wood shavings or plaster etc... falling over you. Apart form wearing goggles to protect your eyes you can catch all the bits that fall by firstly pushing the drill bit through a paper or plastic cup with the open end pointing upwards.

Quick tip

CLEANING SCRAPERS
Rusty scrapers and filler knives are easily cleaned by rubbing with a metal soap pad. Dip the pad into turpentine and rub vigorously. Avoid using water as this will lead to the tools rusting.

Nailing tips

- Dip large nails in paraffin or rub them with soap to help them go in smoothly.

- Try to offset a run of nails along a strip of wood, as keeping to the same grain could cause splitting.

- Use a comb or a piece of cardboard with a v-notch to hold a nail in place whilst hammering. This can save on bruised fingers!

- Before driving nails into plaster, heat them first and they will go in more smoothly.

Tiling tips

- When tiling a bathroom always start on the wall where the bath is.

- For a neat finish, place the cut tiles in a corner so the uncut edge of the tile is next to the adjacent wall.

- When cutting a curved line on a tile, make a template out of a piece of cardboard, place it on the tile and mark with a felt tip pen, then cut with a tile saw.

- Tiling over gloss paint is not recommended as the tiles will only be fastened to the gloss paint and not the wall. Rub down the walls with a rough glass paper to cut through the gloss surface and give the tile adhesive something to grip to.

"Law of the Workshop:
Any tool, when
dropped, will roll
to the least
accessible corner."

Floating floors

- Rather than being nailed or glued to a concrete or plywood sub floor, floating floors, such as laminate flooring, float on top of the sub-floor and should be laid on a moisture resistant membrane specially made for the flooring.

- Floating floors move with changes in humidity in the room where they are installed. Because of this, a small gap is left around the edges, so that such floors will not buckle, crack or squeak.

- You can test a newly laid concrete floor for moisture before laying a floating floor by simply taping a piece of plastic sheet to the floor and leaving overnight.

- If the floor is wet under the plastic when you take it up the next day then it is too wet to lay the floor.

- To make your job easier and quicker hire a compound mitre saw for all the cutting or, better still, buy one to assist with all your other DIY projects as well.

- After you get your packs of flooring home, acclimatise them by stacking them for at least 48 hrs in the room in which they will be laid.

- Open each pack as you go. Allow at least a 12mm gap all around the wall when laying your floor; this allows for expansion which will in turn stop the floor from lifting or buckling up.

Safer drilling

Whenever you have to drill into walls or ceilings use a battery operated wire/pipe detector to avoid drilling into cables or pipes hidden in the wall. Even if you think you know where these are, don't take the risk – you could easily be mistaken and the results could be costly. Pass the cable/pipe detector over the area of wall or ceiling that you are going to drill into to and a visual or audible signal will inform you of the exact position of any hidden services.

Tar on cars

There are a few good ways that you can try to remove tar marks on car paintwork. Rub the marks with margarine, and leave for a few hours before wiping off with a damp, soapy cloth. You can mix bicarbonate of soda with enough water to make a paste and rub this onto the tar mark, which should lift away easily. Finally a few drops of lighter fluid or WD-40 lubricating oil on a soft cloth and rubbed into the tar should also do the trick. After any of the above methods, wax the area.

Clear car windows

On a foggy morning a car's windscreen and windows can continually mist over. Avoid this happening by rubbing a cut, raw potato over the exterior of all the glass. When it dries the window will stay mist free. To keep car windows frost free on an icy morning, coat them the previous night with a solution of three parts vinegar to one part water.

Drilling metal

When drilling into metal always use a slow drill speed and, to avoid any overheating, place putty around the hole and periodically add a few drops of white spirit into the hole for lubrication.

Doorstop

An old wooden cotton reel can be nailed to the floor to act as a doorstop. You can blend it in by painting it to match the colour of the floor covering.

Lop-sided pictures

Avoid the irritation of slipping pictures by wrapping a piece of adhesive tape around the centre of the string or wire on the back of the pictures before hanging.

Filling cracks

If you have mixed your own decorating filler to fill cracks then it can be applied more effectively using an old icing bag rather than trying to force the filler into areas using a pallet knife.

Quick tip

QUICK PLUMB LINE

If you need a plumb line in a hurry and you do not have a proper, shop bought one, then you can easily make one by simply hanging a bunch of keys from a piece of string.

Matching filler

After cutting or sanding wood for a project, collect the sawdust and mix it with PVA glue. You then have a matching pot of wood filler available if ever required. It will keep well in a small, sealed plastic pot.

Ceiling tiles

When putting up polystyrene ceiling tiles there is always a danger of getting finger marks (or even holes!) in them when trying to press them into place. If you use a soft paint roller you can apply even pressure and the problems are avoided.

Horizontal drilling

A useful way of ensuring that your electric drill is perfectly horizontal before drilling into a wall is to place a loose fitting washer over the drill bit. If the washer stays in the middle of the bit then you are drilling straight. If it falls towards the drill or the wall then you are off line!

Damp starting

Damp air on a cold winter morning can give you real trouble in starting the car. If this happens then use a hairdryer to dry out the engine, especially any electrical contacts.

Home security

The key thing to remember about home security is that you should never leave anything to chance, or assume that because you're in the garden, your house is safe. There are a number of precautions you can take and it's worth spending time and money on these before an incident forces you to.

Some small improvements to consider...

- Treat your drainpipes with anti-climb paint (you are legally required to display a warning if you use anti-climb paint).

- If there are external areas of your house that are particularly dark at night, invest in security lights, programmed to stay on for at least 5 minutes.

- Lay an area of gravel pathway or drive, as the noise when walked on helps deter burglars.

- Invest in a burglar alarm – as well as protecting your property, having an alarm can also lower your insurance premiums. It's worth getting professional advice about this to ensure that you choose the right technology for your home and lifestyle.

- Good locks are essential, both on doors and windows. Almost two thirds of burglars gain access through a door. There is a wide variety of locks available, so investigate which type will be right for your doors/windows.

- Fit external doors with a mortice deadlock that carries the British Standard Kite mark. You will need to consider the door surrounds as well and make sure they are sturdy. To find a qualified locksmith visit www.locksmiths.co.uk.

- Make sure all your locks are well maintained and never leave keys in doors or windows, or have them visible.

- Make sure you are not invisible from your neighbours. High walls, fences and hedges mean that if your neighbours can't see in, your home becomes more attractive to burglars.

- If you have a rear boundary that opens onto fields, a footpath, or other open ground then consider planting 'burglar-proof' plants such as pyracantha, holly, hawthorn, berberis or dog roses as a pretty but lethal deterrent!

- Make sure your shed is securely locked. If you have very expensive tools and machinery stored then consider either fitting an alarm or including the shed in your house alarm system if you have one.

- Ensure you lock ladders and any other tools (garden or general DIY) safely away. Don't leave them out for burglars to use to gain entry to your house.

- Keep your holiday plans quiet, cancel your paper and milk deliveries, and ask the Royal Mail to hold your post. Think about timer switches to control lights.

- Ask your local crime prevention officer to arrange a visit to review and advise what steps you can take to improve your security – both inside and out.

- Don't ever leave your house empty without checking that it is properly secured. A two-minute trip to the corner shop is all an intruder could need to get in.

- Consider joining a Neighbourhood Watch scheme or, if you don't already have one running in your area, talking to your neighbours about starting one.

Bolt cutting

If you need to cut a threaded bar or bolt then remember to put the nut on first and screw it on past the place you are going to cut. When you have made the cut take off the nut and it will remove any burred metal with it. If you try to get the nut on after cutting then you may have difficulty.

> ### Quick tip
> **ADHESIVE HANDS**
> After applying any sort of DIY adhesive there is always a chance that some will end up on your hands. This can be removed by dipping your sticky hands into flour. The adhesive will then be much easier to remove and should just peel off.

Stuck nut

If you have a nut that seems impossible to get off, use a blow lamp (if it is safe to do so) to heat the nut for a few seconds. This will expand the metal slightly and, if you are ready with the correct spanner and a hammer, a sharp tap should release the nut.

Plumb line shadow

If you are using a plumb line to get that perfect vertical, maybe for wallpapering, then to avoid marking the wall with a pencil simply shine a bright light on the line and it will cast a perfect shadow. You can then use the shadow line to work to.

Rubbing door

If you find that a door is rubbing a little on the carpet then there is probably no need to remove the door and plane the bottom. Place a surform blade or 60 grit sandpaper rough surface uppermost under the door where it appears to be rubbing and move door quickly backwards and forwards. This should remove just enough of the offending wood to allow the door to swing freely.

Sawing softwood

When sawing softwoods, instead of drawing a line with a pencil or pen, score the wood with a sharp blade such as a craft or Stanley knife. This will cut the fibres in the wood and makes it easier to start the saw and keep to the exact cutting line.

Quick tip

GLUING

When gluing two surfaces together remember the golden rule – "The thinner the glue line the stronger the joint". Achieve this by gently rubbing the two glued surfaces together until they barely move before clamping together.

Plaster seal

When painting new plaster or any similar porous surface first paint on a solution of water mixed with PVA glue. This will seal the surface and stop the paint from soaking into the plaster, making it go a lot further and giving a much better finish.

REMOVING LINOLEUM

If you are trying to remove linoleum and you find that it is stuck fast with glue, then you can make the job easier by using a warm iron and a tea towel. Place the tea towel over the area of linoleum to be lifted and apply the iron over this just for a few seconds. This should melt the glue and enable you to easily pull up the whole piece of linoleum rather than in fragments!

Magnetic cleaning

When drilling a hole into iron or steel you will often find that fine bits of metal can fall in and are difficult to remove. They can, however, be easily removed using magnetism! Simply find a steel or iron rod that will fit into the hole, right to the bottom. Press a strong magnet to the upper end of the rod and, keeping it there, remove the rod. The bits of waste metal will be stuck to the end and can be brushed off.

Leaking car radiator

If you have a leaking car radiator try one of these short term remedies until you can get to a garage. If you can see the leak, then place a piece of chewing gum over the hole; the heat of the radiator will keep the gum tacky and should seal the hole. Alternatively try cracking an egg into the boiling radiator, which should seal the hole from the inside. Be very careful, however, when opening a car radiator cap. Cover with a thick cloth first and open it very slowly to allow the pressurised steam to escape.

Ladder safety

One of the golden rules of ladder work is never to wear slippery soled shoes. Even if you think that the rungs of the ladder have treads that are rough enough to give you a firm footing, don't take chances. One drop of spilled paint or estranged sealant under your feet could be your downfall – literally!

Drilling glass

If you have to drill through a mirror or sheet glass then this procedure will ensure success. First mark the spot for drilling with a felt-tipped pen. Next make a small well of glazing putty and place this over the marked spot so it sticks to the surface but you can still just see the mark. Then fill the well with light oil such as sewing machine oil. Start drilling slowly using a carbide-tipped drill bit. The oil will keep the drill bit cool and prevent the glass from cracking.

Wardrobe doors

When the catches on a wardrobe's doors become worn the doors may be prone to swinging open. A drawing pin, pushed into the top or bottom edge of the offending door or doors will often prove a cost effective solution to the problem!

Coloured filler

If using filler on stained wood or dark hardwood then add a little instant coffee powder to the filler to make the colour a better match. Experiment with different amounts in a small quantity of filler until you achieve a good colour match.

Oil spillages

Immediately an oil spill occurs, in the garage or on the drive, it should be covered with fresh, dry cat litter. This will quickly and easily soak up the oil. When the oil has been absorbed the litter can be carefully swept up and disposed of. More can then be applied if required. Pouring cola over dried oil or grease stains on a brick driveway can usually effect their removal. If the cola is applied in the evening and left overnight, when it is washed off in the morning the stain should have disappeared.

Cleaning guttering

Guttering should be checked and cleaned on a regular basis both that on the house and also on the garage, garden shed or greenhouse. You should be extra vigilant during the autumn when falling leaves can soon block guttering and down pipes and cause major problems. Even if you have no deciduous trees in your own garden you are not safe. There is a little matter of the wind!

Before cleaning gutters place a bowl or bucket under the down pipe. This will prevent any debris from blocking the drains. You may have to remove a section of the down pipe to allow you to take this precautionary measure but it is worth the trouble.

Wearing a good, strong pair of gloves first remove any leaves, twigs etc... from the gutter troughs. A piece of wood the same shape as the curve of the gutter but slightly smaller can be cut and used as a scraper for a thorough job. Then brush the gutters with a stiff brush and hose the remaining debris down into your waiting bowl of bucket.

Filling ceiling cracks

On a largely level and sound surface, ceiling cracks are probably going to be down to expansion or settlement. Often people resort to covering the whole ceiling with lining paper, which doesn't always look great and is literally 'papering over the cracks'! Here's how to fill those ceiling cracks permanently:

Always use a flexible decorator's caulk or gap filler which must be the type that is workable with water and a finger or brush and described as 'permanently flexible'. Never use wall filler for sanding. This will only to sit on the surface and ultimately crack under the same forces as caused the original damage.

- Begin by brushing the cracks with a clean paintbrush to remove all of the loose plaster. Wear safety goggles.

- Next brush undiluted PVA as far into the cracks as you are able to. This will create a sound surface to which the flexible filler can stick.

- Then force a thick line of filler into the cracks so that they are slightly over filled. Work quickly and accurately so that the filler is still workable without water.

- Now take a scraper or putty knife and run it along the raised filler, forcing it deeper into the cracks and then flatting out the surfaces.

- Finally, with a firm paintbrush and water, brush away the filler at the sides of the cracks. Avoid getting water into the crack itself.

- If there are any deep cracks, this final stage may need to be repeated several times.

"Remember –
you cannot hang
everything on
one nail.

Removing skirting board

During some DIY tasks you might need to remove the skirting boards from around the room and refit them. Problems occur if the skirting is old and has dried out making the boards very vulnerable to splitting. The top edge – where you are going to be levering the board from – is also often thinner, moulded and hence easily broken.

The following tip will enable you to remove the board cleanly without splitting:

1. Beginning at one end of a length of skirting board carefully tap a long-handled, broad-bladed screwdriver down behind the board all the way to the floor. This should bring the top edge of the board out about 1.25 cm (½") from the wall, giving you room in which to push to an 45 cm (18") crowbar.

2. Levering off the board with a crowbar would probably still succeed in splitting the edge off. Instead push the crowbar in at 45° of upright and between the shaft of your screwdriver and the wall.

3. Carefully pull on the handle of the screwdriver and ease the crowbar down as far as possible behind the skirting, ensuring that you do not to let it slip out from behind the screwdriver.

4. When it's in as far as it will go, push the screwdriver handle back. The tongue of the crowbar will push against the screwdriver, forcing out the board across the whole height without any splitting.

Repairing decorative plaster cornice and ceiling roses

The job can be made easy by making a simple mould using children's Play Dough, or plasticine as follows:

1. Find an undamaged section of the cornice or ceiling rose, similar to the damaged area, to copy. Without removing any of the old paint, wash this with mild soapy water.

2. Mould the Play Dough over the detail ensuring plenty of coverage, and then make a few finger imprints into the outside of the Play Dough ensuring that you do not go right through.

3. Apply mix of plaster mixed with dirty hot water (this sets much faster!) to the back of the Play Dough mould. This acts as container for the mould. If the mould is quite big then put a layer of scrim cloth in the plaster to prevent cracking.

4. When dry remove the plaster backing carefully and gently remove the Play Dough. Place the plaster container onto a bench and carefully Play Dough back into plaster mould making sure to align the finger imprints.

5. Pour new plaster into the Play Dough mould and leave to dry. For these repair jobs ordinary plaster is fine so don't worry about trying to source specialist plaster.

6. Finally, remove the new plaster-cast detail from the mould, stick into place using Gripfill and paint to match the existing cornice or ceiling rose.

Removing broken glass

If you need to remove a broken or cracked pane of glass then wearing thick, protective gloves and safety goggles is essential before you proceed as follows:

- If the broken pane of glass has a hole in it then gently lever the remaining pieces out, starting at the top.

- If the glass is cracked, but with no pieces missing, you will need to use a glasscutter to cut round the pane, about an inch or so from the frame. Before you do this, place adhesive tape over the cracks in the glass. You can then tap it gently from the inside to separate the pieces one at a time. The tape should help prevent the pieces from dropping out.

- Once broken glass has been removed, use a hacking knife to cut away the old putty. Holding this knife at an acute angle to the frame and tapping it with a hammer and remove the putty without damaging the frame.

- As you work around the frame, you will find the small retaining pins or sprigs in wooden frames or spring clips in metal frames. These can be removed with pincers.

- Using the hacking knife or an old blunt chisel, it is important to remove all the old putty back to the original frame so that the new pane of glass will sit in it correctly.

- Finally dust out the frame rebate and apply a coat of wood or metal primer according to the frame type and allow this to dry.

Damp

There are several factors that can cause damp patches to appear on the inner surface of a wall. By doing a little detective work, it is relatively easy to work out what is causing the problem, and so take appropriate action.

There are some obvious things to check, but frequently these are overlooked...

- Check to see whether there is a nearby downpipe that is fractured or leaking at a joint. This can cause water to drain out of the back of the pipe and down the wall, whilst hidden from general view.

- A similar check can be made of the gutters. They can become blocked by leaves and other debris causing them to overflow. The resulting flow of water over a prolonged period will soon begin to percolate through the brickwork and cause unsightly damp stains on the interior decoration.

- Another common cause of dampness can be plants growing too close to the house. The problem with these is that moisture and rain gets trapped. With little airflow behind to help dry off the moisture when the weather is reasonable, this dampness can quickly become a problem.

- Rising damp is usually easy to recognise. It is given the name because it is caused by moisture being drawn up through the wall from the damp ground below. This is referred to as capillary action. The reason that it does not go higher than about a metre, is that once this height is reached, the weight of water becomes too much for the capillary action to be able to draw it any higher. So, if the damp area is only within the bottom 1 m (3') or so of the wall, it's a sure indication of rising damp. The cause of this is usually one of two things:

The damp proof course (DPC), an impermeable membrane set low down in the wall, may be bridged somewhere. In other words, something is providing a route for the moisture to get past the DPC. Examples of this might be soil in a flower-bed which is too high along the wall, or a patio which has been laid too high, and without due consideration for the DPC. In both cases, remedial action will need to be taken to overcome the problem.

The DPC may have broken down. An example of this might be an old property where slate was used as a DPC, and there has been some movement causing the slate to fracture. Once this has happened, the water can be drawn up into the brickwork above. In some very old properties, there may be no DPC at all. The correct procedure for dealing with a broken DPC is to have either a new section fitted in the area or to have a chemical injected into the wall to make that section impervious. Both these jobs are normally carried out by specialists who should also be able to provide a guarantee on the work.

Fencing tips

A few things to consider when erecting wooden garden fencing:

- Check the condition of garden fences regularly and make any repairs immediately. If you wait, a windy night could make the job twice as big and much more costly.

- Never try to carry out any lasting repairs or erect new fencing in bad weather. By all means take emergency action to temporarily fix the problem but wait until a calm dry day to do it properly.

- Most fencing jobs will require two people. Trying to be a hero on your own could be foolish and lead to injury.

- Always use pressure-treated (also known as 'tanalised') wooden posts as these should carry a guarantee against rot and will last for 10 to 15 years.

- Take the time to run a straight string line to mark the position of the fence run and use a spirit level to check that the posts are vertical and the panels are horizontal.

- Wooden posts can be anchored in place in two ways. You can use either long metal spikes which are driven into the ground and have a square socket at the top to accept the post or by concreting the bottom 450 mm (18″) of the post into the ground. If the soil is loose then always use the concrete option but wait at least a day for the concrete to set.

- Never allow wooden fencing panels to be in contact with the soil as they will eventually rot. If you cannot leave a gap beneath then attach a 150mm (6″) or 300mm (12″) wide, pressure-treated (tanalised) gravel board to the bottom of each panel and let this sit on the soil.

Fixing a leak in a flat roof

You can often extend the serviceable life of a flat roof by carrying out minor repairs yourself. If left unattended, the problems will get worse and the covering will need to be replaced.

- Make sure you have a safe means of access to the roof and take great care when working near the edges. If you have any doubts, or the roof is higher than single storey, get a professional. Also be sure that the roof is capable of supporting your weight.

- Various kits containing special tape and adhesive are available for carrying out patch repairs, which should be done in dry weather.

- Clean the area thoroughly, removing chippings and killing off any mould growth with fungicide.

- If the surface is split, fill the gap with mastic before patching.

- A burst blister should be dried out with a hot air stripper. You might be able to fill in the hole by spreading the warm asphalt with a stripping knife.

- Allow to cool and then prime the surface of the area to be repaired with the special primer supplied.

- Cut the tape to length and press firmly down into place.

- Make sure the edges are well sealed.

- When complete, replace chippings to protect the surface.

If this is not for you, get a quote from a local tradesman. They can often fit in minor repair work between larger jobs. It's always best to get a recommendation – have a word with friends and neighbours.

Patio laying tips

Here are a few useful things to remember when laying slab path or patio:

- When ordering your slabs allow an extra 15% to 20% for breakages or cutting. You can usually strike a deal with the builder's merchant to return any slabs that are unused.

- Make sure that the surface on which you are laying the slabs is solid. If in any doubt then hire a petrol-driven compactor plate to ensure you have a firm foundation on which to lay. If the ground has been recently dug, the house is under 12 months old or you are in any way unsure about the solidity of the ground then dig out 100 mm (4") depth of soil from the area and compact down a mixture of hardcore and sand to the required level.

- Decide whether you are going to lay the slabs on a dry mix of 6:1 building sand to cement or a wet mortar mix of the same ratio. A dry mix is easy to work with and acceptable for areas that will receive light use. A wet mix, although a bit trickier to use, gives a far stronger foundation and should be used if you are in any doubt or for areas of heavy usage.

- If you are laying slabs for vehicle use then you should always lay a 150 mm (6") compacted hardcore foundation layer first and use a wet mortar mix as a bed for the slabs. Make sure the slabs that you choose are recommended for vehicles.

- Whether mixing by hand or using a cement mixer, ensure that the sand and cement are thoroughly mixed otherwise the resulting foundation will not be of uniform strength.

- When making a wet mortar mix, the addition of a small amount of washing-up liquid to the water can help to make the mix smoother and easier to use.

- Only make up enough mix—wet or dry—that you can comfortably use in an hour as the mix will start to 'go off' and will not bond successfully to the slabs.

- Always lay slabs on a full bed of mortar mix. Using a 'five blobs of mortar' technique is false economy as there will always be gaps beneath the slabs. If something heavy is dropped on them there is more chance of them cracking.

- When laying slabs always ensure that there is a slight slope away from the house for the run off (or 'fall') for water to drain away. This only needs to be about 1:50 for smooth faced slabs and 1:40 for more uneven-surfaced or 'rivened' slabs.

- Take your time in laying the slabs and check often with a spirit level that you have the required fall. When first offering the slabs onto the mortar mix they should only require a few taps with a rubber hammer to get them to the correct level. If they look as though they are too proud then lift them and remove some of the mix. Don't be tempted to continue hitting the slab as it will probably break!

- Remember to always leave joints of about 10 mm (3/8") between the slabs. This will allow slabs to be easily lifted should any need replacing. It will also enable you to cope with any slight discrepancies in the sizes of, apparently, similar sized slabs!

- The level of the patio at the house wall must be at least 150 mm (6") below the damp proof course. This is usually visible as an extra wide line of mortar in the brickwork or, in older houses, you may be able to see the edge of pieces of slate that were used. If your patio is built higher than this, the walls will get damp.

- If possible always leave a 50 mm (2") minimum gap between the edge of the patio and the house wall and fill this with gravel. This will ensure that even in the fiercest of storms water will drain away through the gravel.

- For filling in the joints between the slabs you have three choices. You can make up a dry 3:1 mix of building sand and cement and brush this over the surface of the slabs so it fills the joints. The surfaces of the slabs must be perfectly dry to do this as the mix will stick to this and stain damp slabs. Alternatively you could point up the joints using a 3:1 wet mortar mix of building sand and cement. This takes more care but sets quicker and gives a stronger bonding of the slab edges. The final way is to use one of the new air-activated resin jointing compounds such as Geofix. This gives a perfect, hard joint without the difficulties of using wet mortar. It also comes in either grey or buff colours.

Re-skimming old walls

This tip will help you achieve a good, flat plaster finish. Before re-skimming old walls mix a bit of water-based paint in with the Unibond (PVA) prior to plastering. Because you will be able to see uncovered places, this will ensure that you have completely covered the walls and you have left no suction spots that could cause crazing of the new, plaster skimming.

For novice plasterers, a thorough application of a strong PVA mix is essential. It is often recommended on the container to dilute down your PVA with 5 parts water. Don't be tempted to do this, as it will seriously reduce your working time. Two coats of 50:50 PVA water mix will allow you plenty of time to trowel-up your plaster before it goes off and will also help ensure good coverage.

"Be thankful for problems. If they were less difficult, someone with less ability might be doing your job.

Tiling tool kit

- Marking pencil
- Plumb line
- Tape measure
- Spirit Level
- Tile cutter
- Tile nibbler
- Tile saw
- Tile file
- Tile spacers or matches
- Adhesive spreader
- Grout spreader
- Bucket (disposable)
- Hammer
- Cold chisel
- Adhesive
- Grout
- Sponge
- Cleaning cloth

Carpentry tool kit

- Claw hammer
- Tape measure
- Screwdrivers
- Electric drill
- Brace drill
- Wood drill bits
- Utility knife
- Wood chisels (1.25 cm/½″ and 1.9 cm/¾″)
- Mitre box
- Rasps and files
- Clamps
- Sprit level
- Crosscut saw
- Tenon saw
- Plane
- Framing square
- Carpenter's pencil

Bricklaying tool kit

- Bricklayer's trowel
- Bricklayer's float
- Spirit Level
- Builder's square
- String line
- Shovel
- Bucket
- Hammer and bolster chisel
- Measuring tape
- Wheelbarrow
- Pencil
- Builder's spot (board or purpose-made plastic surface on which to mix mortar)

"Keep an odd-sized piece of wood for seven years and you will have a seven-year-old, odd-sized piece of wood."

More tricks
of the trade

chapter 6
More tricks of the trade

Sticking doors and windows

It is really annoying when a newly painted door or window decides to stick. With doors this can be avoided by rubbing the door edges with a candle after the paint has dried and before you try closing the door. A film of talcum powder around the door edge can have the same effect.

For windows you should allow the paint to dry thoroughly and then spray both painted edges with furniture polish. Rub this gently with a soft cloth before closing the windows.

Quick tip

STRONGER SANDPAPER
Sand and emery paper can be made stronger and thus will last longer if you criss-cross the back of the sheets with masking tape.

Steel wool gives a fine finish

To give a really perfect fine surface to decorative wood try using fine steel wool as the final 'sanding' before varnishing. Go about the job gently and work along the grain of the wood. If you go across the grain you will invariably make scratches on the wood.

Smooth bath sealant

To achieve an even, smooth finish when resealing around a bath, put on a rubber glove and dip your fingers in warm, soapy water. Run a soapy finger along the newly-applied sealant whilst applying even pressure. An equally good way of getting a nice finish is to level the sealant with an ice cube.

Quick tip

LADDER MARKS

If you need to lean a ladder against a wall or window frame where it could leave visible marks then avoid this problem by slipping an old sock over the ends of the ladder before use.

More efficient radiators

Because radiators are positioned next to a wall some of the heat will be adsorbed into the wall itself. You can increase the amount of heat radiated into the room by fixing sheets of thick aluminium foil onto the wall behind the radiators with the shiny surface outward. Heat is effectively reflected back off the foil into the room.

Tidy sandpaper

To keep all your wayward pieces of sandpaper and emery cloth in one place use an old clipboard with a thick piece of cardboard placed on top as a cover to prevent the sheets from curling.

Slipping screwdriver

Trying to insert a screw into an awkward place can be a tricky job. To make it easier, put a small piece of putty or Blu-Tak onto the screw head first. The screwdriver is then less likely to slip.

Memorable measurements

When doing DIY tasks, avoid the need to find something to write measurements on by sticking a strip of masking tape onto your ruler or measuring tape. When the job is done remove the masking tape and discard, but put on a fresh piece ready for next time.

Seasoned putty!

Freshly applied window putty is very attractive to birds as they love the taste of the linseed oil it contains. They will think twice about eating it if you mix a little black pepper with the putty before you use it!

Cheap picture hangers

When hanging a lightweight fixture on the wall, instead of searching around for the elusive small picture hook, try stapling, taping or gluing a ring pull from a drink can to the back of the fixing and hanging it from a small nail in the wall.

Metal lubrication

Put a drop of turpentine or vinegar onto the drill bit when drilling into hard metal; it will act as an effective lubricant and make the job a smoother task.

VARNISH ON SKIN

Use nail varnish remover to effectively remove wood varnish from your hands without leaving your skin smelly or dry.

Emergency filler

If you have some small cracks or holes to fill before painting and you don't have any filler then use toothpaste. Allow to dry, smooth off gently with sandpaper and paint as normal. No one will ever know!

Clear drains

Lingering waste that might block up an outside kitchen drain can be shifted with the boiling water used to cook potatoes. If you get into the habit of disposing of your potato water in this way then your drains will always run clear.

Cutting plywood

When sawing plywood, prevent it from splitting by sticking a piece of masking tape over the area to be cut. The tape can be marked with a cutting line using a pencil or fine marker pen.

Sticking drawers

Rubbing the end of an old candle along sticking drawer runners and the drawer itself will grease and lubricate the moving parts. The drawer should then move effortlessly!

Secure hammer handle

To ensure that a new hammer handle is installed securely, before inserting into the hammer head cover the end of the shaft with epoxy resin glue.

Vinyl floor tiles

Removing vinyl floor tiles can be made much easier by using aluminium kitchen foil. Place the foil over the tile to be removed then move a hot iron around slowly on top of the foil. The tile will gradually become unstuck and can be lifted away.

Smoother filler

When mixing wall filler add a few drops of washing-up liquid to the powder and water mix and it will be much smoother and easier to apply.

Screw security

If you have screws that you know you will never have to remove and, for security reasons, you don't want anyone else to be able to either, simply drill out the top of the screw slightly with a high speed steel metal drill.

Quick tip

HANDY SCRAPER

If you need a sharp scraper to remove flecks of dried paint from glass, for instance, then you can easily make one using a razor or Stanley knife blade held in the 'jaws' of a large bulldog stationery clip.

Homemade rubber mallet

If you need a rubber mallet in a hurry, create a temporary one by making a small hole in a tennis ball and pushing this over the head of an ordinary, metal hammer.

Cutting worktops

Whenever you need to cut a wooden kitchen worktop do so from the top using a jigsaw with a blade that only cuts on the downward stroke, not both ways. This will ensure that the top cut edge of the worktop does not become chipped.

Glue pen

A neat little glue brush for fine or inaccessible gluing jobs can be made using the plastic casing of a ballpoint pen and a piece of string. After removing the ink refill from the pen thread the string through the pen's plastic casing. Finally tease out the ends of the string to make the glue brush bristles.

Rubber-backed carpet

If you are laying rubber-backed carpet or underlay onto a tiled floor, first cover the tiles with newspaper or brown paper. This will prevent the rubber from sticking to the tiles, an advantage should you ever want to change the floor covering.

Cutting marble

Amazingly you will find that marble is not much harder than oak and can be cut by using an ordinary panel saw and re-sharpening often during the cutting.

"By the time a man realises his father was right he has a son who thinks he's wrong."

Long timber cuts

When sawing down a long length of timber, cut small wedges out of scrap timber and insert these periodically into the cut as you progress. This will help to stop the saw blade from jamming.

Quick tip

LEAKY WATERING CAN
If you do not possess a soldering iron, a small hole in a galvanised watering can easily is repaired by sealing it with enamel paint.

Wallpapering with wood-chip

If you are papering a wall with wood-chip paper and intend to paint over it afterwards then tear the sides of each strip of paper. This way no seams will show through after painting.

Split tool handles

If you have a wooden handled tool that has the beginnings of a split along its length then an emergency repair can be made using one or two jubilee clips of the correct diameter. If this works and you don't mind the look – it could end up as a permanent repair!

Foam cutting

Foam rubber that needs to be cut into shape for seating can be difficult to cut smoothly. Use an electric carving knife to make the job smoother and quicker. It does no harm at all to the knife.

Floorboard gaps

Gaps between floorboards can be filled by mixing an amount of wallpaper paste to a very stiff consistency and adding shredded brown paper. Fill the gaps with the mixture and leave slightly proud of the floor. When dry, sand, stain and seal to match the other floorboards.

Smoother sawing

A wood saw will cut through timber a lot smoother and without snagging if the teeth of the saw are first rubbed with soap.

Brass screws

When screwing brass screws into hardwood first coat the screw with soap or candle wax. This will lubricate the screw and stop the screw head from snapping off. You could also drill a very fine pilot hole into the wood first, which makes inserting the screw easier and safer.

Stronger joints

When gluing a wooden joint sprinkle a few strands of fine steel wool on one of the glued surfaces before joining; this will produce a much stronger bond.

Sink blockages

When you are clearing a blockage in a sink, basin or bath with a plunger then use a damp cloth to cover the overflow before you begin plunging. This will increase the pressure and your efforts will be more effective.

Cutting pipes

To cut a pipe perfectly square without having to mark around the pipe with a pen, simply place a piece of paper around the pipe so that the edges are lined up and use this as a guide for the hacksaw.

Cellar steps

If you have cellar steps to paint add a little sand to the paint before use; you will give the painted treads a rough feel and hence a much better grip. As most cellar stairs are pretty steep, it is a good safety tip.

Fake ebony

If you need a small piece of ebony to make a repair and can't get hold of any then don't despair. You can cheat by obtaining an equivalently sized piece of beech or deal and standing this in a strong solution of ordinary black tea for about three weeks. The result is a piece of fake ebony!

Quick tip

SCRATCH FREE

Always keep your safety goggles on the workbench inside an old cotton sock. This will stop the lenses from getting scratched.

Emergency Rawlplugs

These can easily be made from small pieces of plastic clothes line with the wire removed, empty plastic pen casing, or pieces of tightly rolled cardboard.

Large nuts and no spanner?

Use a metal, carpenter's G-clamp tightened around the nut. Then gently tap this with a hammer.

Small nuts, large spanner?

Place a coin of the appropriate width between the jaw of the spanner and the nut. Be careful not to deface the coin, though, as you could be in legal trouble!

Patterned glass replacement

To avoid the possibility of injury, take a rubbing of the patterned glass to the glaziers rather than a piece of broken glass.

Removing tight screws

If you need to remove a tight old screw successfully first apply paint remover to screw head. Secondly soak the area with vinegar and wait for about an hour. Finally place a good fitting screwdriver in slot and strike firmly with a hammer before turning and removing with ease.

"Never put off till
tomorrow what
you can put off
till the day after.

Oozing joints

When gluing joints together, run a strip of masking tape along the edges of the joint so any excess glue will ooze out onto the tape, which can then be easily and cleanly removed.

Plier marks

The jaws of pliers are made for gripping and can leave permanent marks. To avoid this happening, either cover the jaws with masking tape or cut the fingers from an old pair of gloves and pull these over the jaws.

STOP PADLOCK FREEZING
To stop an outside padlock from freezing up during the winter, wrap it in cooking foil with the shiny side outwards.

Choked drill bits

If your drill bit becomes clogged when drilling wood or masonry then simply have a small wire brush to hand. Reverse the drill and touch the bit with the wire brush.

No fine sandpaper?

Simply use wire wool or a green kitchen scourer.

Sweeping fine dust

If you need to sweep up fine dust then, no matter how careful you are you will invariably get clouds of it filling the air. To avoid this, sprinkle with water before starting.

Marking timber

If you need to mark cutting lines in timber and don't want to see the remains of a pencil line afterwards, then use a sharp knife instead.

Quick tip

DRESS LIKE A BUILDER
Without a doubt you will always get a better deal from the local builder's merchants if you go in actually looking like a builder! Paint-splattered jeans, old check shirt, boots and a pencil behind your ear will often do the trick. The same applies to the gents too!

Slipping screw

If you have a screw that is constantly slipping then wind fuse wire around thread or force a matchstick down the side of the screw when screwing back in.

Homemade lubricant

If you need a lubricant in an emergency then try lard, butter, chalk, candle wax, pencil lead, cooking oil, baby powder or soap. They will always get you out of trouble!

TOOL CARE

Always handle your tools with care – regardless of how hurried you are. Throwing tools into a tool-box can nick or dull their edges and make them difficult to find. Discipline yourself or you can guarantee that the chisel you really need will be the one with the blunt edge.

And finally...

Probably the best bit of DIY advice you could ever receive is 'measure twice – cut once!' Even if you are sure that the measurement that you have just taken is correct, take it again – just to be sure!

"Glass, china and reputation are easily cracked, but never easily mended."

Wood, glass, screws & nails

chapter 7
Wood, glass, screws & nails

Wood types:

Hardwoods

These include Ash, Beech, Cherry, Chestnut, Elm, Lime, Mahogany, Oak (English, Japanese and other imported), Rosewood, Teak and Walnut.

Hardwoods are strong and more expensive than softwoods because of their durability and longevity. They are ideal for making good quality furniture and flooring. The wood is seasoned to strengthen it and should have been covered during storage.

Softwoods

These include Cedar, Deal, Hemlock, Larch, Pine, Spruce, Redwood, Whitewood and Yew.

Softwoods may be cheaper than hardwoods but they will not last as long, especially outside. For exterior use they require regular treatment with paints or preservatives to protect the wood from the weather – rain and sun. Softwood can easily become split or warped in storage so check carefully before you purchase.

Sawn or planed?

Sawn timber appears rough as it comes directly from being cut into sections. It is cheaper than planed timber and can be used where its rough appearance cannot be seen, such as in a loft space for rafters and joists.

Planed timber has been machine cut and planed to give a smooth edge. It is slightly more expensive than rough-cut timber but can usually be painted or stained immediately without further sanding.

Block-board

This is made by the high pressure bonding of glued rectangular strips of softwood sandwiched between a veneer of wood such as birch. If the block-board has a single veneer on each side it is called 3-ply or, if it has a double veneer to each face, 5-ply. As the glues used to make block-board are not waterproof it should only be used inside. Painting should be done to each side to retain the tension and shape of the board.

Chipboard

This is made from particles of softwood coated in resin, spread over a flat plate and heat-bonded under high pressure. There are various grades of chipboard — flooring, melamine veneered (Formica), plastic veneered and wood veneered.

Hardboard

This is made by forcing softwood pulp into sheets which, for the standard hardboard sheet, are smooth finished on one side and textured on the other. There are other types of hardboard available – duo faced, medium, oil-tempered, painted, plastic faced and perforated (pegboard).

MDF

MDF stands for Medium Density Fibreboard and is an extremely versatile timber product suitable for a wide variety of interior DIY projects. It cannot be used outside or allowed to get wet. It is made by bonding wooden fibres together under high pressure in a way that gives a very fine texture throughout t he timber. As the fibres used are extremely fine it is important to use a face mask when cutting MDF to avoid inhaling the dust particles.

Plywood

This is made by bonding veneers together, face-to-face, with the grains running in alternate directions. Sheets are always bonded either side of a central sheet to keep the tensioning equal. Therefore the thinnest plywood will be made from three sheets of veneer and is known as 3-ply. Thicker and hence stronger plywood is made by adding sheets equally to both sides of 3-ply to make 5-ply, 7-ply etc... There is a more expensive, waterproof type of plywood available for external use.

Types of glass

There are a number of different types of glass available, in a range of patterns and tints. It is important to decide which is most suited for the particular job in hand.

'Ordinary' sheet glass

This glass is made by passing the molten glass through rollers. The process gives an almost flat finish but the effects of the rollers makes some distortion of the glass inevitable. The glass can be used in domestic windows etc. but the relatively low cost of float glass (with its lack of distortion) has meant that ordinary sheet glass is now used primarily for glazing greenhouses and garden sheds where any minor visual distortions do not matter.

Sheet glass can be cut with a glass cutter and no special equipment is necessary.

Energy efficient glass

Float glass can also be manufactured with a special thin coating on one side, which allows the suns energy to pass through in one direction while reducing heat transfer in the other direction.

The special, energy efficient coating often gives the glass a very slight brown or grey tint. The coating is not very strong and does not last long if subjected to normal cleaning or external weather conditions. This type of glass is, therefore, normally only used in sealed double (or triple) glazed units where the special coating is on the inside.

Float glass (plate)

This glass gets its name from its method of manufacture. Molten glass is 'floated' onto a bed of molten tin. This produces a glass that is flat and without any visual distortions. Float glass can be cut using a glasscutter and is suitable for fixed and opening windows above waist height.

Patterned

Made from flat glass, this has a design or pattern rolled onto one side during manufacture. It can be used for decorative effect as well as to provide privacy.

Patterned glass is available in a range of coloured tints as well as plain. Each pattern design normally has a quoted distortion number, from 1 to 5, 1 being very little distortion, 5 being a high level of diffusion. On external glazing, the patterned side is usually on the inside so that dirt can easily be removed from the flat external face.

Laminated glass

Laminated glass is made up of a sandwich of two or more sheets of glass bonded together by a flexible, normally transparent material.

If the glass is cracked or broken, the flexible material is designed to hold the glass fragments in place. The glass used in the sandwich can be any of the other basic types (float, toughened, wired etc.) and they still retain their original breaking properties. Some laminated glass provides decorative internal finishes to the glass while others act as fire breaks.

"It's a small world,
but I wouldn't like
to paint it.

Toughened (safety glass)

Toughened glass is produced by applying a special treatment to ordinary float glass after it has been finished and cut to size. The treatment involves heating the glass to about 620°C so that it begins to soften followed by rapid cooling. This produces a glass that, if smashed, breaks into small pieces without any sharp edges. The treatment does, however, increase the surface tension of the glass that can cause it to 'explode' if broken but this is more of a dramatic effect than hazardous.

Toughened glass is ideal for glazed doors, low level windows and for tabletops, where it can withstand high temperature associated with cooking pots etc. The treatment to produce toughened glass must be applied only after all cutting and processing has been completed, as once 'toughened', any attempt to cut the glass will cause it to shatter.

Wired glass

This type of glass incorporates a wire mesh (usually with about 10mm spacing) in the middle of the glass. If the glass cracks or breaks, the wire tends to hold the glass together. It is ideal for roofing in such areas as a garage or conservatory and is available as clear or obscured. Wired glass is not considered a safety glass as the glass still breaks with sharp edges.

Picture frame glass

Glass available specifically for picture framing tends to be referred to as 'diffused reflection' glass. They have high transparency but low reflective properties to reduce reflections when the picture or photograph is viewed.

Mirrors

Mirrors are usually made from 4-6mm thick float glass which has been silvered on one side. Mirrors without a surrounding frame are made from a type of safety glass. Old mirrors, and modern mirrors supplied within a frame, should never be used unframed as any damage to them might cause the glass to shatter into dangerous fragments.

Screw types:

Single-slot countersunk head screws

These are traditional screws with a long shank and single slot for use with a flat-head screwdriver. They are used for general joining work and hinges. 'Countersunk' means that the screw head is shaped so that it can be driven in flush with the surface of the wood etc.

Cross-head, countersunk screws

These are probably the most popular types of screw. These have a cross-shaped slot for the corresponding cross-head screwdriver. This prevents the screwdriver slipping. Philips screws have a slightly different shaped cross-head which lends itself more to driving with a powered screwdriver.

Round-head screws

When these screws are driven in the domed screw head rests on the top of the surface and are easier to remove later if required. They are used to fasten metal to wood, metal to metal or other material. Round-head screws are completely threaded from point to head and the threads are sharp.

Mirror screws

These are most commonly used for fixing mirrors and come in two parts. First there is a countersunk, slotted-head screw which is fixed first. A dome-shaped, chrome cover is then fitted into the top of then screw for a decorative finish.

Chipboard screws

These are similar to the traditional countersunk type of screw but they have a deeper thread to give a better grip into chipboard.

Twin-thread screws

These screws have two deep threads interwoven with each other. This feature, coupled with a narrower shank, give the screws a much better grip.

Self-tapping screws

These are used in tougher materials such as metal and fibreglass. To use self-tapping screws, a pilot hole that is the same gauge of the shank of the screw must first be drilled into the material. As the screw is tightened into the material it cuts a thread.

Clutch-head screws

The heads of these screws have a unique cross pattern which allows the screws to be tightened but not undone. They are used in situations of security such as when fitting locks etc... It is best to use an ordinary screw of the same size first, whilst doing the initial fitting of equipment. This will enable you to make any minor adjustments to the fitting before using the permanent clutch-head screw.

Dry-wall screws

These are thinner than normal screws and have much sharper points. The thin screw heads enable them to be driven easily into the surface of the board or studwork.

Screw measurements

A wood screw is always labelled with two measurements – the screw length and the shank diameter. The length is measured from the tip of the screw to the part of the screw that will eventually be level with the surface of the wood. A gauge number is given to the shank to indicate its diameter i.e 6, 8, 10. The higher the shank number the thicker the screw.

Nail types:

Round wire nails

These general purpose nails with a large, round, flat head are mostly used for rough carpentry where appearance is not important but strength is essential. They are inclined to split a piece of wood. Sizes are ¾" to 6" (20mm-150mm).

Oval wire nails

The heads of these nails can be easily hidden by knocking them below the surface using a nail punch. This makes them most suitable for joinery work where appearance is important. They are less likely to split the wood if driven in with the longer sides parallel to the grain. Sizes are from 12mm-150mm (½"-6").

Round or lost-head nails

These are similar but stronger than oval wire nails. They can easily be punched below the surface of the wood. Sizes are from 12mm-150mm (½"-6").

Galvanised nails

These zinc-coated nails are rust-proof and hence very useful for exterior use.

Hardboard nails

These nails have diamond-shaped heads which are virtually hidden when hammered into hardboard. They are used frequently in carpentry. Sizes are from 9mm-38mm (3/8"-1½").

Masonry nails

These are rectangular, with an L-shaped head and are nearly always used for nailing floorboards to joists. Sizes are from 25mm-150 mm (1"-6").

Square twisted nails

These comparatively expensive nails offer a more permanent, screw-like grip than plain nails. They have shanks with a spiral twist so they work like screws and twist into the wood.

Annular nails

These nails are useful where very strong joints are required. The sharp ridges round the shanks become embedded in the wood to give a tight grip.

Cut clasp nail

These nails are rectangular in section. Once used they are extremely difficult to remove and hence provide a very strong fixing in wood and pre-drilled masonry. Sizes are from 1″ to 6″ (25mm -150 mm).

Clout head nails

These are made of galvanized steel, with a large, flat retaining head. This nail is most suitable for soft materials such as plasterboard and roofing felt.

Spring-head roofing nails

These special nails are used for fixing corrugated sheeting to timber. The twisted shank and inverted cup head produces a very strong purchase.

Panel pins

Small, round, lightweight nails used for cabinet-making, fixing small mouldings and other fine carpentry work.

Tacks

Short nails with a wide, flat head, used for fixing carpets to floorboards and for stretching fabric on to wood and other upholstery work.

Sprigs

These are small nails without heads. They are used mainly to hold glass in window frames before applying putty which covers them up. Sizes are from ½″ to ¾″ (12mm - 19mm).

Upholstery nails

These are available in chrome, brass and other metallic finishes. They are used as secondary fixings with tacks. The dome heads gives a decorative finish when finishing upholstery work such as nailing chair coverings into place. Various head sizes are available.

Staples

These are U-shaped round wire nails with two points to hold lengths of wire in position. Some staples have an insulated lining for fixing flex and electric cable.

As you slide down the banister of life, may the splinters never point in the wrong direction.

Calculators & conversion charts

Wallpaper calculator

Distance around room		Height of room		
(m)	(ft)	2.15–2.30m (7–7.5ft)	2.30–2.45m (7.5–8ft)	2.45–2.60m (8–8.5ft)
9 m	29.5 ft	4	5	5
10 m	33 ft	5	5	5
12 m	39.5 ft	5	6	6
13 m	42.5 ft	6	6	7
14 m	46 ft	6	7	7
15 m	49 ft	7	7	8
16 m	52.5 ft	7	8	9
17 m	56 ft	8	8	9
19 m	62.5 ft	8	9	10
20 m	65.5 ft	9	9	10
21 m	69 ft	9	10	11
22 m	72 ft	10	10	12
24 m	77 ft	10	11	12
25 m	82 ft	11	11	13
26 m	85.5 ft	12	12	14
27 m	88.5 ft	12	13	14
29 m	95 ft	13	13	15
30 m	98.5 ft	13	14	15

When choosing wallpaper always check the batch/shade numbers are the same. Make sure you buy enough wallpaper to finish the job. Any unopened rolls can be returned for a refund. This chart is for guidance only. For large patterned wallpaper you will need to allow extra rolls for matching.

The distance around the room includes windows and radiators and the wall height is from skirting board.

Tile calculator

Tile size		Quantity required	
Metric (mm)	Imperial (in)	per sq. metre	per sq. yard
100x100	4″ x 4″	100	84
108x108	4.25″ x 4.25″	86	72
150x150	6″ x 6″	44	36
200x100	8″ x 4″	50	41
200x150	8″ x 6″	33	27
200x200	8″ x 8″	25	20
225x150	9″ x 6″	29	24
225x225	9″ x 9″	20	16
250x150	10″ x 6″	27	22
250 x150	10″ x 10″	16	13
250x250	12″ x 8″	17	14
300x200	12″ x 12″	11	9
300x300	13″ x 13″	9	8

This chart might help you when buying tiles. Remember to buy some extra just in case you suffer breakages.

Conversion charts

WEIGHT & MEASURE CONVERSIONS

Length:		
1 millimetre (mm)		= 0.0394 inch (in)
1 centimetre (cm)	= 10 mm	= 0.0394 in
1 metre (m)	= 100 cm	= 1.0936 yard (yd)
1 kilometre (km)	= 1,000 m	= 0.6214 mile

1 inch		= 2.54 cm
1 foot (ft)	= 12 in	= 0.3048 m
1 yard	= 3 ft	= 0.9144 m
1 mile	= 1,760 yd	= 1.6093 km

Area:		
1 square cm (cm^2)	= 100 mm^2	= 0.1550 in^2
1 square m (m^2)	= 10,000 cm^2	= 1.1960 yd^2
1 square km (km^2)	= 100 hectares	= 0.3861 $mile^2$

1 square in (in^2)		= 6.4516 cm^2
1 square ft (ft^2)	= 144 in^2	= 0.0929 m^2
1 square yd (yd^2)	= 9 ft^2	= 0.8361 m^2
1 acre	= 4,840 yd^2	= 4,046.9 m^2
1 square mile	= 640 acres	= 2.590 km^2

Volume:		
1 cubic cm (cm³)		= 0.0610 in³
1 cubic decimetre (dm³)	= 1,000 cm³	= 0.0353 ft³
1 cubic m (m³)	= 1,000 dm³	= 1.3080 yd³
1 litre (l)	= 1 dm³ = 1000 millilitre = 2.113 US pt	= 1.76 pint (pt)
1 hectolitre (hl)	= 100 l	= 21.997 gallon = 26.417 US gallon

1 cubic in (in³)		= 16.387 cm³
1 cubic ft (ft³)	= 1,728 in³	= 0.0283 m³
1 cubic yd (yd³)	= 27 ft³	= 0.7646 m³
1 fluid ounce (fl oz)		= 28.413 ml
1 pint (pt)	= 20 fl oz	= 0.5683 l
1 gallon (gal)	= 8 pt	= 4.546 l = 1.201 US gallon

Mass:		
1 milligram (mg)		= 0.0154 grain
1 gram (g)	= 1,000 mg	= 0.0353 ounce (oz)
1 metric carat	= 0.2 g	= 3.0865 grains
1 kilogram (kg)	= 1,000 g	= 2.2046 pound (lb)
1 tonne (t)	= 1,000 kg	= 0.9842 ton

1 oz	= 437.5 grains	= 28.35 g
1 lb	= 16 oz	= 0.4536 kg
1 stone	= 14 lb	= 6.3503 kg
1 hundredweight (cwt)	= 112 lb	= 50.802 kg
1 ton	= 20 cwt	= 1.016 t

Index

'The Greatest Tips in the World' books

Pet Recipe books

The Greatest Feline Feasts in the World by Joe Inglis
ISBN 978-1-905151-50-9

The Greatest Doggie Dinners in the World by Joe Inglis
ISBN 978-1-905151-51-6

'The Greatest in the World' DVDs

The Greatest in the World — Gardening Tips
presented by Steve Brookes

The Greatest in the World — Yoga Tips
presented by David Gellineau and David Robson

The Greatest in the World — Cat & Kitten Tips
presented by Joe Inglis

The Greatest in the World — Dog & Puppy Tips
presented by Joe Inglis

For more information about currently available
and forthcoming book and DVD titles please visit:

www.thegreatestintheworld.com

or write to:

The Greatest in the World Ltd
PO Box 3182
Stratford-upon-Avon
Warwickshire CV37 7XW
United Kingdom

Tel / Fax: +44(0)1789 299616
Email: info@thegreatestintheworld.com

The author

Chris Jones' interest in DIY started at the age of 6 when he took up the parlour parquet flooring with his first tool kit! He qualified as an electrician over 20 years ago and had a successful electrical contracting business for 14 yrs. Chris worked as a demonstrator and adviser for a major DIY store. You may have even seen him on TV! Chris is the real 'family man' and is passing on his DIY knowledge and vast experience to his boys Peter & Mark helped by the endless patience of his wife Cathy.

Brian Lee trained as a decorator 35 years ago. After 9 years in the army, Brian developed a passion for crafting useful things out of wood. His job now involves teaching DIY skills (mainly to ladies and children!) with bird tables, nesting boxes and dovecots often being on his project list. Born in Cheshire but now living in Hampshire with his wife Yvonne, Brian is keen to pass on his great DIY know-how to his three grown up children and two grandchildren.